MW00710566

The North America Sylva V1: Or A Description Of The Forest Trees Of The United States, Canada And Nova Scotia

Francois Andre Michaux

THE
NORTH AMERICAN
SYLVA,

OR

A DESCRIPTION OF THE FOREST TREES

OF THE

UNITED STATES, CANADA AND NOVA SCOTIA,

Considered particularly with respect to their use in the Arts,
and their introduction into Commerce;

TO WHICH IS ADDED

A DESCRIPTION OF THE MOST USEFUL OF THE EUROPEAN FOREST TREES.

ILLUSTRATED BY 156 COLOURED ENGRAVINGS.

Translated from the French of

F. ANDREW MICHAUX,

Member of the American Philosophical Society of Philadelphia; Correspondent of
the Institute of France; Member of the Agricultural Societies of Charleston, S. C.,
Philadelphia and Massachusetts; Honorary Member of the Historical, Literary and
Philosophical Societies of New York.

..... *arbore sulcamus maria, terrasque admovemus,*
arbore exædificamus tecta.

PLINII SECUNDI: *Nat. Hist.*, lib. XII.

VOL. I.

PARIS,

PRINTED BY C. D'HAUTEL.

1819.

TO

JAMES HILLHOUSE,

LATELY A SENATOR

OF THE

UNITED STATES,

THIS WORK IS INSCRIBED,

BY

HIS AFFECTIONATE FRIEND AND OBEDIENT SON,

AUGUSTUS L. HILLHOUSE.

PREFACE.

THE Author of the *North American Sylva* has made me the most grateful return in his power, for the pains I have bestowed upon his publication, by requesting me to dedicate it to my father.

No literary pretensions, I am sensible, can be founded on a labour imperfectly executed, and so humble in its kind, that perfection itself would be without praise. I should not have attached my name to the part which I first translated, nor to the work thus entire, but for the pleasure which I was assured it would afford a revered parent, to whom my obligations exceed the common measure of filial gratitude. In the performance of so extended a task he will discern proofs of that perseverance which is the basis of every valuable character; and in the usefulness of the work, an apology for my diversion from more appropriate pursuits.

The departures that may be observed from the sense of the original are in compliance with notes of the author: with more leisure I could have rendered my style less faulty. I have not escaped the use of impure idioms, which I was studious to avoid. American writers should labour assiduously to weed from their dialect all the peculiarities which are unauthorized by taste — not from deference to the critics, but to the laws of criticism. Our language, in its purity, is copious and flexible enough to be always susceptible of accuracy and grace.

The author of this valuable work will, I hope, be induced to complete it by a practical treatise on the formation and management of forests. That branch of economy, which is admirably developed in France and Germany, must soon command attention in the United States. Though three fourths of our soil are still veiled from the eye of day by primeval forests, the best materials for building are nearly exhausted : with all the projected improvements in our internal navigation, whence shall we procure supplies of timber, fifty years hence, for the continuance of our marine? The most urgent motives call imperiously upon the government to provide a seasonable remedy for the evil: from a government like ours, which is the faithful expression of the public will, and which has no concern but the prosperity and honour of the nation, prospective wisdom is reasonably demanded.

I have no pecuniary interest in this publication, and may therefore express my solicitude for its success. Mr. Michaux—actuated no doubt by a mixed motive—desirous of rendering his name familiar to a people whom he respects, and anxious to possess them of a body of information which he justly considers as of great practical utility, has executed this edition at an expense which ill comports with the modest fortune of a man of letters. It would not become us to accept such a present from an individual. While we allow Education among ourselves to loiter in the porch of Science, and consent to receive from strangers that knowledge of our own country which they should receive from us — for our reputation — let us, at least, reward their services.

Besides his personal merit, the Author of the *Sylva* has hereditary claims upon our gratitude.

A. L. H.

Citizen of the United States.

Paris, 20 May, 1819.

INTRODUCTION.

T**HE** researches of learned botanists for more than a century past have shown how highly the North American Continent is favoured in its vegetable kingdom. But their object seems to have been rather the progress of botanical knowledge, and the embellishment of European gardens, than an acquaintance with the properties of the American plants and with the uses of the forest trees. This, on the contrary, was the end which I had particularly in view in my travels in the United States in 1807; and the work which I offer to the public is the fruit of my inquiries.

Before entering into any details concerning the plan which I have adopted, it should be remarked that the species of large trees are much more numerous in North America than in Europe : in the United States there are more than 140 species that exceed 30 feet in height, all which I have examined and described; in France there are but 30 that attain this size, of which 18 enter into the composition of the forests, and 7 only are employed in building.

To collect information, it was necessary for me
to visit different parts of the United States. Beginning at the District of Maine, where the winter is as
long and as rigorous as in Sweden though 10 degrees farther south, I travelled over all the Atlantic
States, in some of which the heat during six months
is nearly as great as in the West Indies. Besides a
journey of 1800 miles from north-east to south-west,
I made five excursions into the interior parts of the
country; the first, along the rivers Kennebeck and
Sandy, passing through Hallowel, Winslow, Nor-
ridgewock and Farmington; the second, from Boston to Lake Champlain, crossing the States of New
Hampshire and Vermont; the third, from New York
to the Lakes Ontario and Erie; the fourth, from
Philadelphia to the borders of the rivers Mononghahela, Alleghany and Ohio; and the fifth, from
Charleston to the sources of the Savannah and
Oconee. In travelling along the sea-coast, I visited
the principal ports to examine the timber employed in ship-building, and entered work-shops of
every description where wood is wrought. The
knowledge of which I stood in need was principally
in the possession of mechanics; accordingly, I consulted the most skilful workmen, natives of the

country and Europeans, and by means of a series of questions previously prepared, collected, for the benefit of the United States as well as of Europe, a mass of information which I trust will be found in the main correct.

In proceeding southward, I noted exactly the disappearance of some species of trees and the appearance of others, according to the changes of climate or of soil.

I have pointed out the trees which form an object of commercial exchange between the Middle, Northern and Southern States, or are sent to the West Indies and to Great Britain; the parts of the country which produce them, and the ports from which they are exported; the different kinds of wood employed for fuel, for enclosing fields, and in the mechanical arts; the sorts of bark used in tanning, etc.

I have endeavoured, also, to impress on the American farmers the advantage of preserving and multiplying some species and of destroying others; for, in my opinion, a bad tree should not be suffered to exist where a good one might grow, and in no country is selection more necessary than in North America.

It may not be improper to observe that the Euro-

peans have great advantages over the Americans in
the management of woods. The principal forests are
in the hands of the governments, which watch over
their preservation with a solicitude dictated by im-
perious necessity. Experience has amply demons-
trated that no dependance can be placed, for the
public service or the general supply, upon forests
that are private property : falling sooner or later
into the hands of persons eager to enjoy their price,
they disappear and give place to tillage. In America,
on the contrary, neither the federal government nor
the several States have reserved forests. An alarm-
ing destruction of the trees proper for building has
been the consequence — an evil which is increasing
and which will continue to increase with the increase of population. The effect is already very
sensibly felt in the large cities, where the complaint
is every year becoming more serious, not only of
the excessive dearness of fuel, but of the scarcity of
timber. Even now, inferior wood is frequently substituted for the White Oak; and the Live Oak, so
highly esteemed in ship-building, will soon become
extinct upon the islands of Georgia.

Though the English language is almost universally
spoken in the United States, yet their extent and

their settlement at different periods have created a singular confusion in the nomenclature of trees: the same species has different names in different places, or even in the same district; and the same name is given to very different species. I have carefully collected these denominations, omitting such as are rarely employed.

I have described only those species which have been observed with attention by my father and myself. This remark is the more necessary, as the nurseries and gardens of Europe contain trees said to have come from North America, which neither he nor myself were fortunate enough to find. In several botanical works, also, trees are mentioned as species, which we discovered to be mere varieties. This last observation is particularly applicable to the *Flora of North America,* by Pursh, published in London in 1814. Several Oaks, designated in it as species, I am confident will be found, on further examination to be varieties resulting from a difference of soil and climate. I have, however inserted extracts from such articles in that work as are not contained in my own. Allowances I hope will be made for the occasional freedom of my remarks upon botanical writers, who, from the want of personal examination, have given erroneous accounts of the trees of North America, or unfavourable opinions of their timber : my object has been to lead to a more minute examination, and thus to an ultimate correction of error wherever it may be found.

At the close of the work will be placed a complete and particular recapitulation of the various kinds of wood used in different parts of the United States in the mechanical arts and for fuel, with a general index of the vulgar and scientific names.

In this first English edition important improvements have been made, particularly by inserting descriptions and drawings of several trees, such as the Yellow Wood of Tennessee and the Ohio Buckeye, of which I had not seen the flowers : of these species the seeds which I brought from the United States in 1803 have grown up and bloomed since the publication of my work. I have, besides, added descriptions and figures of the trees which principally compose the European forests and which are the most commonly employed in building, pointing out those which might be advantageously propagated in the United States. The Chesnut, the Beech and the Hornbeam are omitted, because their perfect re-

semblance in aspect, foliage and fruit to the analogous American species rendered a separate figure
unnecessary.

I flatter myself that the course I have pursued in
the execution of this task will be found more prac-
tically useful, and consequently more generally
interesting, than if I had followed a more scientific
path. I have been anxious to render my work ac-
ceptable to the great body of American agricultur-
ists, to the farmers of the Northern and the planters
of the Southern States. It will afford me sincere grat-
ification if I succeed in obtaining the approbation
of the liberal and enlightened men by whom I was
encouraged during my residence in the United States.

Public acknowledgments are due for the assistance
which I received from Dr. H. Muhlemberg, one of
the most learned botanists that America has produced, who deserved a distinguished place among
the most eminent in that pleasing science in Europe;
from Mr. W. Hamilton, an enlightened lover of the
arts and sciences, who took pleasure in collecting,
at his magnificent seat (the Woodlands) near Philadelphia, such vegetables of the United States and
of other countries as are useful in the arts or in med-
icine; and from Mr. W. Bartram, known equally

for his travels and his various knowledge in natural history, and for the amiability of his character and the obliging readiness with which he communicates to others the result of his researches. •

To the pupils of the late professor B. S. Barton, professor D. Hosack and Dr. Bigelow, animated like their masters with an ardent desire for the advancement of Natural History, I leave the task of completing my work, and of offering to their fellow-citizens a treatise on this interesting subject more worthy of their acceptance.

THE
NORTH AMERICAN
SYLVA.

~~~~~~

·OAKS.

In the greater part of North America, as well as in Europe, there is no tree so generally useful as the Oak. It is every-where the most highly esteemed in the construction of houses and of vessels, and is commonly selected for implements of husbandry. It seems, also, to have been multiplied in proportion to its utility : without insisting upon the diversity of climates to which it is indigenous, we may observe that the number of its known species is already considerable and is daily increasing, particularly on the Western Continent, and that its varieties are infinite. These considerations determined my father, in 1801, after his return from the United States, to publish a Treatise containing drawings and descriptions of the Oaks of that country, which was favourably received by the lovers of botany and agriculture.

The following extract from his work exhibits a just outline of this tree: " The genus of the Oaks (*Introduct.*

I. 2

p. 4.) comprises many unknown species; most of those
which grow in America exhibit such various forms
while young, that they can be ascertained with certainty
only when arrived at maturer years. Often an intermediate variety so nearly resembles two species, that it
is difficult to determine, from the foliage, to which of
them it belongs. Some species are so variable, that it is
impossible, by the leaves, to recognize their identity in
youth and at a more advanced age. Others are so similar,
that specific characters must be derived from the fructification, which is itself liable to variations and exceptions. It is only by a comparison of stocks of different
ages that analogous species can be distinguished, and
varieties correctly referred to their species.

" I have endeavoured to arrange the American Oaks
in a natural series, the characters of which I first sought
in the fructification : but this afforded only unimportant
distinctions, such as the position of the barren flowers,
whether pedunculated or nearly sessile, and the size
and period of the fruit. Neither was I able to found
my distinctions on the structure of the cup : I was
obliged, therefore, to have recourse to the foliage,
which has been made the basis of a division into two
sections, the first containing the species with beardless
leaves, and the second, those in which the summit or
lobes are terminated by a bristle.

" The interval between the appearance of the flower
and the maturity of the fruit is different in different

species; and this distinction I have admitted as a secondary character.

" All the Oaks are proved to be monœcious. We know too that on the European White Oak and other species, the female flowers are situated above the male upon the shoots of the same season ; that both are axillary; and that, immediately after the fecundation, the male flowers fade and fall, while the female blossom continues advancing through the natural stages, till, in the course of the year, it ripens into perfect fruit. But there are some species whose fertile flowers remain stationary a whole year, and begin to develope their germ the second spring, probably because they are not fecundated the first season; so that eighteen months elapse between the appearance of the flower and the maturity of the fruit. Hence I have formed a subdivision into species of annual and species of biennial fructification. The female flower which is axillary the first season, ceases to be so of course at the falling of the leaf. Several species are found upon the Old Continent whose fructification is biennial, such as the Cork Oak, *Quercus suber*, etc."

I have derived great assistance from my father's work, and have adopted his arrangement, which perfectly accords with my own observations. But I have inserted several new species , and have suppressed two that were not well ascertained : the existence of one of them is doubtful, and the other is evidently a duplicate.

What chiefly distinguishes my work from his, is the
more extended practical observations; which are the
fruit of my own researches. My constant aim was to ap-
preciate the utility of each species in the mechanical
arts, and to point out those which are the most deserving of attention in Europe and America. If in this respect I have some advantage, my father's work will always preserve its title to the attention of botanists and
amateurs of foreign plants, by other details not con-
sistent with my plan. They will find, for example, quo-
tations from all the authors who had previously taken
notice of the species he describes, and in the plates,
leaves of the young plant as well as of the full-grown
tree.

I have described twenty-six American species, which
I have divided into two sections, according to the term
of fructification : the first comprising ten species that
bear fruit every year ; and the second, sixteen of which
the fructification is biennial. I have learned by multiplied
observations that, with the exception of the Live Oak,
the wood of the first section is of a finer texture, more
compact, and consequently more durable.

Linnæus, in the third edition of his *Species Plantarum,*
published in 1774, described fourteen species of Oak,
of which five only are natives of the New World.
Since that period such additions have been made to
the list, that the new edition of Willdenow's *Species
Plantarum* published in 1805, contains forty - four

American species; of which sixteen were recognized by Messrs. Humboldt and Bonpland in Old Mexico, and twenty-six by my father and myself in the United States and the adjacent countries. Probably the American series will be still farther augmented by discoveries in the western part of Louisiana, and in the interior provinces of New Spain, a country 1200 miles in extent lying between the United States and Old Mexico, which no naturalist has explored.

In America, as we have just observed, are found forty-four species, which are all comprised between the 20th and the 48th degrees of north latitude; in the Old Continent are enumerated only thirty, which are scattered on both sides of the equator, beginning at the 60th degree north.

This sketch is not without utility, and appears naturally in this place ; such parallels might perhaps contribute more than is generally thought to the progress of botany and agriculture, and they deserve particular attention from naturalists travelling in foreign countries. It would be interesting to possess comparative tables of those plants which are found in the higher latitudes of both Continents, and of the trees and shrubs of the temperate climates of America with the analogous species found in nearly the same latitude in Asia. I have long entertained a wish, which will doubtless be shared by all who interest themselves in the science , that botanists would go more deeply into the geography of plants. The rapid progress of the young Americans who are beginning to devote themselves with ardour to the study of Natural History, will soon afford the requisite information concerning their own portion of the globe.

METHODICAL DISPOSITION

OF THE OAKS

OF NORTH AMERICA,

INCLUDING THREE EUROPEAN SPECIES.

Monœcia polyandria. LINN. *Amentacœ.* JUSS.

FIRST DIVISION.

Fructification annual.

FIRST SECTION.—*Leaves lobed.*

1. White Oak. . . . . . Quercus alba.
2. Common European Oak Quercus robur.
3. European White Oak. . Quercus robur pedunculata.
4. Mossy-cup Oak. . . . Quercus olivœformis.
5. Over-cup White Oak. . Quercus macrocarpa.
6. Post Oak. . . . . . . Quercus obtusiloba.
7. Over-cup Oak. . . . . Quercus lyrata.

SECOND SECTION.—*Leaves toothed.*

8. Swamp White Oak. . . Quercus prinus discolor.
9. Chesnut White Oak. . Quercus prinus palustris.
10. Rock Chesnut Oak. . . Quercus prinus monticola.
11. Yellow Oak. . . . . . Quercus prinus acuminata.
12. Small Chesnut Oak. . . Quercus prinus chincapin.

SECOND DIVISION.

Fructification biennial; leaves mucronated. (except in the 13th species.)

FIRST SECTION.—*Leaves obtuse or entire.*

13. Live Oak. . . . . . . Quercus virens.

14. Cork Oak. . . . . . . *Quercus suber.*
15. Willow Oak. . . . . . *Quercus phellos.*
16. Laurel Oak. . . . . . *Quercus imbricaria.*
17. Upland Willow Oak. . *Quercus cinerea.*
18. Running Oak. . . . . *Quercus pumila.*

SECOND SECTION.—*Leaves lobed.*

19. Bartram Oak. . . . . *Quercus heterophylla.*
20. Water Oak. . . . . . *Quercus aquatica.*
21. Black Jack Oak. . . . . *Quercus ferruginea.*
22. Bear Oak. . . . . . . *Quercus banisteri.*

THIRD SECTION.—*Leaves multifid or many-clefted.*

23. Barren Scrub Oak. . . *Quercus catesbæi.*
24. Spanish Oak. . . . . . *Quercus falcata.*
25. Black Oak. . . . . . . *Quercus tinctoria.*
26. Scarlet Oak. . . . . . *Quercus coccinea.*
27. Grey Oak. . . . . . . *Quercus ambigua.*
28. Pin Oak. . . . . *Quercus palustris.*
29. Red Oak. . . . . . . *Quercus rubra.*

WHITE OAK.

QUERCUS ALBA. *Q. foliis subæqualiter pinnatifidis; laciniis oblongis, obtusis, plerumque integerrimis; fructu majusculo; cupulá crateratá, tuberculoso-scabratá; glande ovatá.*

THROUGHOUT the United States and in Canada, this tree is known by the name of *White Oak*. The environs of the small town of *Trois Rivières* in Canada, latitude 46° 20′, and the lower part of the river Kennebeck in the District of Maine, are the most northern points at which it was observed by my father and myself. Thence we traced it along the sea-shore to a distance beyond cape Canaveral, latitude 28°, and westward from the Ocean to the Country of the Illinois, an extent of more than 1200 miles from north-east to south-west, and nearly as much from east to west. It is, however, by no means equally diffused over this vast tract; in the District of Maine, Vermont and Lower Canada, it is little multiplied, and its vegetation is repressed by the severity of the winter. In the lower part of the Southern States, in the Floridas and Lower Louisiana, it is found only on the borders of the swamps with a few other trees which likewise shun a dry and barren soil : this region is generally so sandy that it is covered with a continued growth

I.   3

of Pines, as will be more particularly mentioned in
the description of the Long-leaved Pine. The White
Oak is observed also to be uncommon on lands of extraordinary fertility, like those of Tennessee, Kentucky
and Gennessee, and of all the spacious vallies watered
by the western rivers. I have travelled whole days in
those States without seeing a single stock, though the
few that exist, both there and in the Southern States,
exhibit the most luxuriant vegetation.

The White Oak abounds chiefly in the Middle States
and in Virginia, particularly in that part of Pennsylvania
and Virginia which lies between the Alleghanies and the
Ohio, a distance of about 150 miles, beginning at Brownsville on the Mononghahela. Near Greensburgh, Maconel-
ville, Unionville and Washington Court-house, I have
seen large forests, nine tenths of which consisted of
White Oaks whose healthful appearance evinced the favourable nature of the soil, though in general they were
not more than 15 inches in diameter. East of the mountains this tree is found in every exposure, and in every
soil which is not extremely dry or subject to long inundations; but the largest stocks grow in humid places.
In the western districts, where it composes entire
forests, the face of the country is undulated, and the
yellow soil, consisting partly of clay with a mixture of
calcarious stones, yields abundant crops of wheat.

By the foregoing observations it appears that the severity of the climate, the fertility of the soil, its dryness

or humidity, are the causes which render the White
Oak so rare over three quarters of the United States that
it is inadequate to supply the local demand, though the
country does not contain a fourth of the population
which it is capable of supporting.

Among the American Oaks this species bears the
greatest analogy to the European Oak, especially to the
variety called European White Oak, *Quercus peduncu-*
lata, which it resembles in foliage and in the qualities
of its wood. The American White Oak is 70 or 80 feet
high, and 6 or 7 feet in diameter ; but its proportions
vary with the soil and climate. The leaves are regularly
and obliquely divided into oblong, rounded lobes, destitute of points : the sections appeared to be the deepest
in the most humid soils. Soon after their unfolding they
are reddish above and white and downy beneath ;
when fully grown they are smooth and of a light green
on the upper surface, and glaucous underneath. In the
fall they change to a bright violet colour, and form an
agreeable contrast with the surrounding foliage which
has not yet suffered by the frost.

This is the only Oak on which a few of the dried leaves
persist till the circulation is renewed in the spring. By
this peculiarity and by the whiteness of the bark, from
which it derives its name, it is easily distinguished in
the winter. The acorns are of an oval form, large, very
sweet, contained in rough, shallow, greyish cups, and
borne singly or in pairs, by peduncles 8 or 10 lines in

length, attached, as in all the species with annual fructification, to the shoots of the season.

The fruit of the White Oak is·rarely abundant, and
frequently for several years in succession a few handfuls
of·acorns could hardly be collected in a large forest
where the tree is multiplied. Some stocks produce acorns
of a deep blue colour ; but I⁴have found only two individuals of this variety, one a flourishing tree in the garden of Mr. W. Hamilton near Philadelphia, and the
other in Virginia.

The trunk is clad in a white bark, which is often variegated with large black spots. On stocks less than 16
inches in diameter the epidermis is divided into squares ;
on old trees, growing in moist grounds, it is in the
form of plates laterally attached. The wood is reddish,
and very similar to that of the European Oak, though
lighter and less compact, as may be proved by splitting
billets of each of the same size: in the American species
the vessels which occupy the intervals of the concentrical circles are visibly less replete. But of all the American
Oaks which I shall describe, this is the best and the most
generally used, being strong, durable, and of large dimensions. It is less employed than formerly in building
only because it is scarcer and more costly.

At Philadelphia, Baltimore, and in the smaller towns
of the Middle States, the frame of all well built houses,
whether of brick or wood, is of White Oak. West of the
Alleghanies, where Pine boards are not easily procured,

the White Oak is substituted for the floors and for the
exterior covering of the frame, notwithstanding its liability to warp and split.

It is much used in the construction of mills and dams,
particularly for such parts as are exposed to be alternately wet and dry.

The wooden bridge nearly 3000 feet long that unites
Boston and Cambridge, is supported by posts of White
Oak, from 16 to 20 feet in length, which have replaced
those of White Pine on which it originally stood.

The excellent properties of this wood cause it to be
preferred for a great variety of uses, among which are
many articles manufactured by the wheel-wright. This
trade is carried to the greatest perfection at Philadelphia,
and its wares are highly esteemed for solidity both at
home and abroad. White Oak perfectly seasoned is employed for the frame of coaches, waggons and sledges,
for the mould board of ploughs, the teeth of wooden
harrows, the felloes and spokes of wheels, particularly
the spokes of coach-wheels. In the Northern, Middle
and Western States, the naves are also made of Oak
in the country; but it splits too easily to be proper for
this object. Except in the District of Maine, it is always chosen for the bow or circular back of windsor-
chairs. The wood of the young stocks is very elastic and
is susceptible of minute division, hence it is preferred
for the large baskets used in harvesting, for the hoop of
sieves, the bottom of riddles, and the handles of coach-

whips which are braided and covered with leather; at
Boston it is chosen for pail-handles, and in Maine, for
axe-helves.

In many parts of the Middle States, the White Oak
is selected for the posts of rural fence, and beyond
Laurel-Hill in Pennsylvania, where it is common, it
forms the entire enclosure.

The bark is considered by many tanners as the best
for preparing leather for saddles and other similar objects; it is little employed however, because in the
United States the bark of the trunk and large limbs only
is employed; and on these the cellular integument is
much thinner in the White than in the Red Oak, which
is besides more abundant.

I have been told that the bark yields a purple dye :
though I have not witnessed the fact, I am disposed to
believe in its existence, as I received the information
from persons residing several hundred miles from each
other. But if the colour was not defective in perma-
nence or intensity, it would have found its way into
commerce, like the *Quercitron* of the Black Oak.

Of all the species that grow east of the Mississippi, the
White Oak alone furnishes staves proper for containing
wine and spirituous liquors. The domestic consumption
for this purpose is immense, and vast quantities are
exported to the West Indies, Great Britain, and the
Islands of Madeira and Teneriffe. The Post Oak might
indeed be applied to the same use, but even in Mary-

land and Virginia, where it is most common, it is not sufficiently multiplied to supply the local demand.

The Rock Chesnut Oak and the Swamp White Oak in the Northern and Middle States, the Chesnut White Oak and the Over-cup Oak in the South, are compact enough to prevent the escape of spirits and fine oils, yet porous enough to absorb them. If they united every requisite quality, and were employed for this purpose, they would be consumed in less than ten years.

It is well understood at Bordeaux that the wood of the European White Oak is closer grained than that of the American species, and the preference is given to our domestic growth or to that imported from Dantzick. The American Oak is exclusively employed in Madeira and the West Indies only because it is cheaper and more easily procured.

White Oak staves are exported from all the ports of the Northern and Middle States, and from New Orleans. Those which come from Baltimore, Norfolk and New Orleans, are far superior to those of the Northern States : the difference results naturally from that of the soil and climate.

The quantity of Oak staves exported to England and the West Indies appears, by two official documents that I have examined, to be considerable. In 1808, the value received by England, amounted to more than 146,000 dollars, and the number of staves sent to the West Indies exceeded 53 millions. I am unable to fix the pro-

portion of the two species of White and of Red Oak;
probably more of the first are sent to England, and of
the second to the Colonies. The price of both has varied
surprisingly within a hundred years : in 1720, staves for
barrels were sold at Philadelphia at 3 dollars a thousand;
in 1798, at 18 dollars; and in 1808, at 30 dollars. In
August 1807, before the American Embargo, they were
advertised at 55 dollars, and in April 1808, after that
municipal regulation became known, at 100 dollars.

The young White Oak, on account of its elasticity,
is very proper for hoops; but it has less strength and
less durability than the Hickory.

Among the uses of this wood, the most important is
in ship-building. In all the dock-yards of the Northern
and Middle States, except in the District of Maine, it is
almost exclusively employed for the keel, and always
for the lower part of the frame and the sides : it is preferred for the knees when sticks of a proper form can
be found. In the smaller ports south of New York, the
upper part of the frame is also of White Oak; but such
vessels are less esteemed than those constructed of
more durable wood.

At Boston, the *trunnels*, or the pins by which the
side-planks are attached to the ribs, are of this species.

To obtain correct notions on the comparative value
of the American White Oak and the European Oak, I
consulted French, English and American ship-wrights,
in almost all the ports of the United States : they

generally agreed that the European Oak was tougher and more durable from the superior closeness of its grain, but that the American species was more elastic and required a shorter time with only half the weight to bend it. This advantage, though important in ship-building, does not compensate for the openness of its pores. Experience, however, every day shows that by growing in places long inhabited its quality is improved; and if the American vessels are less durable than those built in Europe, it is because the timber is not thoroughly seasoned.

The greater part of the immense quantity of White Oak exported from the United States is sent to England. It is shipped only from the Northern and Middle States, in the form of boards and of square timber : what goes to England from Quebec is brought from the shores of Lake Champlain, for Canada probably furnishes hardly enough for its own consumption.

By an extract from the custom-house books of St. John, which I have already quoted, 143,000 cubic feet of Oak wood appear to have entered by this port during the first six months of 1807. Oddy, in his *Treatise on the Commerce of Europe*, says, that in the English dock-yards the White Oak from British America is esteemed excellent timber. This opinion, simply considered, is correct; but that which comes from Baltimore and Philadelphia must still be superior.

Before I conclude this article, I must be allowed to

hasard a conjecture on the consequences of the neglect of all means of preserving and multiplying this tree in the United States; consequences which neither the federal government nor the States have taken any measures to prevent. From the increase of population, and from the impoverishment of the soil produced by a gradual change in the climate, the White Oak will probably, in less than 50 years, be the most rare in the Middle States, where it is now the most abundant; and in Tennessee, Kentucky, Gennessee and farther north, where it is the least multiplied, it will be the most common, and will replace the species which now compose the forests, but which the soil will then be too feeble to sustain. Thus, near the river Kennebeck, in the midst of the primitive forests composed of the Beeches, the Canoe Birch, the Sugar Maple and the Hemlock Spruce, I have observed small tracts, formerly cleared and since abandoned, which are naturally repeopled with the White and Grey Oaks; and in the lower part of Virginia, poor Red Oaks, Yellow Pines and Loblolly Pines are extensively replacing trees of a better quality. East of the mountains, the vallies that lie along the rivers are, with a few exceptions, the only places where the Oak could be advantageously reared; but these fertile lands are more profitably devoted to husbandry.

The American White Oak cannot, in my opinion, be regarded as an useful acquisition to the forests of Europe. Its elasticity, which renders the young stocks proper for

P. J. Redouté del.

White Oak.
Quercus alba.

hoops, is doubtless a valuable property; but the Chesnut of France is superior for this purpose, because it is more durable.

The White Oak is used in the royal dock-yards of England probably because it has been found impossible to procure supplies of European Oak. Perhaps it is employed only for the lower part of the frame, while the European Oak is reserved for the upper timbers.

If the advantage in this comparison be allowed to be on the side of the European species, the Americans should lose no time in introducing it into their forests. To corporations particularly, whose property is less frequently alienated, I take the liberty of addressing this advice, which, if followed, would be productive of great advantage to themselves and to the public. The analogy of the climates leaves no doubt of the perfect success of this tree in the United States, an example of which is found in the garden of Messrs. J. and W. Bartram, 3 miles from Philadelphia, where there is a large stock. which has yielded seed for several years, and which continues to expand with vigour.

PLATE I.

A branch with leaves and acorns of the natural size.

COMMON EUROPEAN OAK.

QUERCUS ROBUR. *Q. foliis petiolatis, oblongis, glabris, sinuatis; lobis rotundatis; fructibus oblongis, sessilibus.*

To the particular attention bestowed upon this interesting tree in modern times is owing its division into two species, the Common European Oak, *Quercus robur*, and the European White Oak, *Quercus pedunculata*. These two species, which are much alike and are usually considered as the same, grow in the same countries, and frequently together. They constitute the greater part of the European forests, from the 6oth to the 35th degree of north latitude, overspreading a great part of the north of Asia and the northern extremity of Africa. They are most abundantly multiplied on the shores of the Black Sea, in Germany, England, France and some parts of Italy, where the climate is particularly favourable to their growth.

The Common European Oak is from 6o to 8o feet in height, numerously ramified, and crowned with an ample and majestic summit. The bark upon the trunk is thick, and upon old stocks, deeply furrowed. The leaves are petiolated, smooth, and of an uniform colour on both sides, enlarged towards the summit, and very coarsely toothed. The acorns are oval and *sessile*, which is the principal difference between the two species.

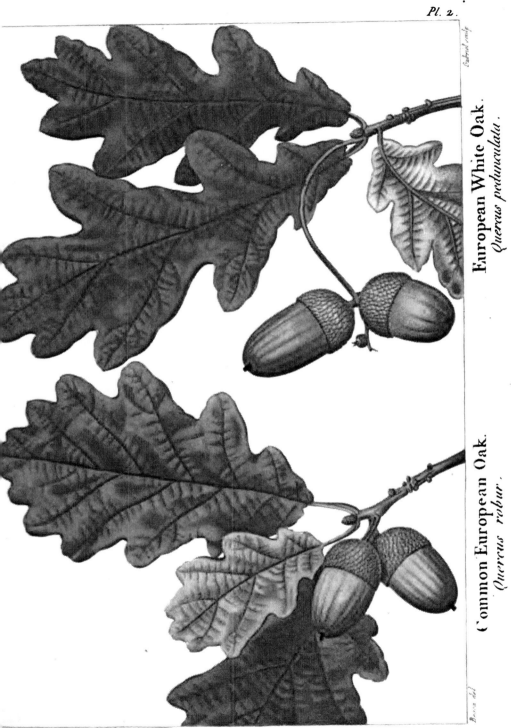

Pl. 2.

Bruce del.

Gabriel sculp.

Common European Oak.
Quercus robur.

European White Oak.
Quercus pedunculata.

This tree prefers high places and the declivities of hills, with a barren gravelly soil; hence it grows more slowly, and its wood is more compact, tougher and heavier than that of the European White Oak. It is less used for household stuff and other kinds of joinery, because it is less easily wrought; but is more esteemed for building and for works that require great strength and durability.

The Common European Oak is subdivided into many varieties, the most valuable of which are the European Black Oak, *Quercus robur lanuginosa,* and the *Quercus robur glomerata.* The first is only 30 or 40 feet high, with small, thick leaves, very downy underneath; its timber is compact and excellent for fuel. The second never rises to a great height; the leaves are small, but smooth on both sides; the acorns are of an inferior size and collected in clusters upon a short common peduncle.

PLATE II.

A branch of the Common European Oak with leaves and acorns of the natural size.

EUROPEAN WHITE OAK.

QUERCUS PEDUNCULATA. *Q. foliis subsessilibus, glabris, sinuatis; fructibus oblongis, pedunculatis.*

THE European White Oak grows of choice in rich bottoms, where the soil is deep and moderately humid. It reaches the height of 90 or 100 feet, and has a large well proportioned trunk, which is often undivided for a considerable distance, and which spreads into a large commanding summit. The bark upon the body is very thick, and on old trees, deeply furrowed; upon the limbs and the young stocks it is greyish, smooth and glossy. The leaves are of a light green on the upper surface, whitish beneath, widened towards the summit, deeply sinuated with blunted points, and supported by short petioles like those of the American White Oak. They are more or less divided according to the age of the tree and to the moisture of the soil. A part of the dry discoloured foliage persists through the winter and falls the ensuing spring.

Besides the difference of the foliage, this species is constantly distinguished from the preceding by its fruit, which is supported singly or in pairs by slender peduncles 2, 3, or even 4 inches long. The acorns are of an oval shape, from 9 to 18 lines in length, according to the age and vigour of the tree, and contained in shallow cups : they fall about a fortnight before those of the Common Oak.

The wood of the European White Oak is of the same colour with that of the American species, the sap being white and the heart reddish; but the texture is closer and the pores fuller, which is probably the reason of its being less elastic, but stronger and more durable. It is more generally esteemed than the Common Oak as it furnishes larger timber, splits more regularly, and is more easily wrought; hence it is preferred for the construction of houses and ships, and is extensively employed by the joiner, the cartwright and the cooper.

Throughout Europe, except in the north of Russia, the bark of the Common Oak and the White Oak is almost exclusively used in tanning. That which is taken from the branches and from small stocks is preferred, because the epidermis is thinner, and the cellular integument, which contains the tannin, more abundant.

Oak wood is more generally used in Europe than in the United States, where the different species of Ash, Birch, etc., in some measure supply its place. The European White Oak would be a valuable addition to the American forests, and I have sent out acorns to begin the formation of nurseries.

PLATE II.

A branch of the European White Oak with leaves and acorns of the natural size.

MOSSY-CUP OAK.

Quercus olivæformis. *Q. foliis oblongis, glabris, subtus glaucis, profunde inæqualiterque sinuato-lobatis; fructu ovato; cupulâ profundius crateratâ, superne crinitâ; glande olivæformi.*

I have observed this species of Oak only in the State of New York on the banks of the Hudson above Albany and in Gennessee, where it is so rare that it has hitherto received no specific name.

Its leaves are of a light green above and whitish beneath : they resemble those of the White Oak in colour, but differ from them in form, being larger, and very deeply and irregularly laciniated, with rounded lobes so various in shape that it is impossible to find two leaves that are alike. The acorns are of an elongated oval form, and are enclosed in cups of nearly the same configuration, of which the scales are prominent and recurved, except near the edge, where they terminate in slender flexible filaments : from this peculiarity I have derived the name of *Mossy-cup Oak*.

This tree is 60 or 70 feet in height, with a spacious summit and an imposing aspect. The bark is white and laminated; but the tree is chiefly remarkable for the form and disposition of its secondary branches, which are slender, flexible, and always inclined towards the

Mossy Cup Oak.

Quercus olivæformis.

earth. This peculiarity alone would render it a valuable acquisition for parks and gardens.

As I have met with this species only in uninhabited places, I have had little opportunity of examining its wood; as far as I can judge, it is not better than that of the White Oak, though far superior to that of the Red Oak.

PLATE III.

Leaves of the natural size. Fig. 1, *An acorn with the cup. Fig.* 2, *An acorn without the cup.*

———

OVER-CUP WHITE OAK.

QUERCUS MACROCARPA. *Q. foliis subtomentosis, profunde lyratimque sinuato - lobatis, obtusis ; fructu maximo ; cupulâ profundius crateratâ, supeine crinatâ ; glande turgide ovatâ.*

THIS interesting species is most multiplied beyond the Alleghanies, in the fertile districts of Kentucky and West Tennessee, and in Upper Louisiana near the Missouri. It is called by the Americans Bur Oak and Over-cup White Oak, and by the French of Illinois, *Chéne à gros gland.*

It is a beautiful tree more than 60 feet in height, laden with dark tufted foliage. The leaves are larger than those of any other Oak in the United States, being frequently 15 inches long and 8 broad : they are notched near the summit, and deeply laciniated below. The acorns, which are also larger than those of any other American species, are oval and enclosed for two thirds of their length in a thick rugged cup, bordered with fine flexible filaments. Sometimes, however, in compact forests, or in very temperate seasons, the filaments do not appear, and the edge of the cup is smooth and bent inwards.

The fructification of this tree is not abundant, and as its wood is inferior to that of the White Oak, it is little esteemed in the United States.

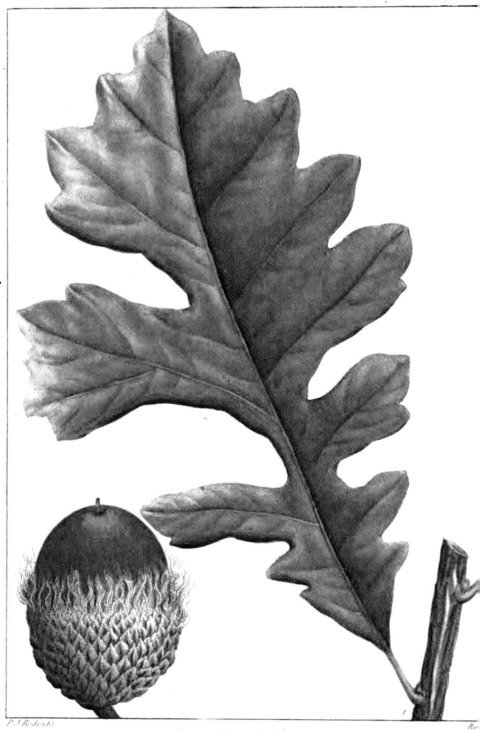

Over Cup White Oak.
Quercus macrocarpa.

I have observed, as well as my father who first made the remark, that the young branches are frequently covered with a yellowish fungous substance, like those of the Elm and Sweet Gum.

PLATE IV.

A leaf of half the natural size. Fig. 1, *An acorn in the cup, of the natural size.*

POST OAK.

QUERCUS OBTUSILOBA. *Q. foliis sinuatis, subtus pubescentibus, lobis obtusis, superioribus dilatatis, bilobis; fructu
mediocri; glande brevi-ovatâ.*

Quercus stellata, WILLD. Sp. Pl.

IN New Jersey near the sea, and in the vicinity of
Philadelphia, this species is thinly disseminated in the
forests, and has hitherto been considered as a variety of
the White Oak. In Maryland and a great part of Virginia,
where it abounds and where its properties are better
understood, it is called Box White Oak, and sometimes
Iron Oak and Post Oak. The last denomination only is
used in the Carolinas, Georgia and East Tennessee.

The steep banks of the Hudson, nearly opposite to
the city of New York, are the most northern points at
which I have observed it. Even here its existence seems
to be secured only by the influence of the sea-air, which
tempers to a certain degree the severity of the winter.
A little farther inland it is not found in the forests. In
the vicinity of South Amboy, 3o miles nearer the sea,
where the soil is dry, and sandy, it is more multiplied,
and it becomes still more vigorous and more common in
advancing towards the south. Westward in Pennsylvania
I saw the last individual of this species a little beyond
Carlisle on the road to Pittsburgh, 15o miles from Philadelphia. Near Baltimore, at the distance of 21o miles

from New York, it abounds in the woods, and attains
its utmost expansion. In Kentucky and Tennessee it is
rare, except on the edges of the swamps enclosed in the
forests, about which it is multiplied though not fully
developed. It probably exists in Lower Louisiana, for
we met with it in East Florida, of which the climate is
the same.

But it is no where more abundant than in Maryland
and in Virginia, between the Alleghanies and the sea.
Wherever the soil is dry, gravelly and unsubstantial, it
forms a considerable proportion of the forests, which
are composed principally of the Black, Scarlet, Spanish
and Black Jack Oaks, the Dogwood and the Yellow Pine.
These woods exhibit a squalid appearance, occasioned
not only by the sterility of the soil, but by the injury they
are constantly sustaining from the cattle which range
through them at all seasons, and which in the winter
are compelled, by the want of herbage, to subsist upon
the young sprouts and the shoots of the preceding
year. The upper part of the two Carolinas and Georgia,
particularly where the Pine and Oak forests unite, is
analogous in soil to that portion of Virginia of which
we have been speaking, and abounds in the Post Oak;
but nearer the sea the barren wastes are covered with
the Long-leaved Pine, and the Oak is seen only in the
lowest parts of the swamps, about the plantations, and
on tracts that have been exhausted by cultivation and
abandoned.

The leaves are borne by short petioles, and are divided into four or five rounded lobes, of which the two nearest the summit are the broadest; they are coriaceous, of a dusky green above and greyish beneath. Towards the fall the ribs are of a rosy tint, instead of a purplish red like those of the Scarlet Oak. The fructification seldom fails. The acorns are small, oval, and covered, for a third of their length, with a slightly rugged greyish cup. They are very sweet, and form a delicious food for squirrels and wild turkeys; hence the tree is sometimes called *Turkey Oak.*

The height of this species rarely exceeds 40 or 50 feet, with a diameter of 15 inches. Its summit, even when compressed in the forests, is disproportionately large, owing probably to the early division of the trunk into several limbs, with which the secondary branches form more open angles than is common on other trees. The branches also are bent into elbows at certain distances, which gives so peculiar an appearance to the tree that it is easily distinguished when the leaves are fallen. The bark upon the trunk is thin and of a greyish white. The wood is yellowish, with no tinct of red. Growing upon a less humid soil, it is less elastic, but finer-grained, stronger and more durable, than the White Oak : hence it is preferred for posts, and is used with advantage by wheel-wrights and coopers.

In ship-building it is used principally for the knees, and is admitted into the lower part of the frame. It rarely

P.J Bedoute.   Re...

Post Oak.
Quercus obtusiloba.

furnishes side-planks or timber of considerable length ; for this reason it is less esteemed than the White Oak, and it is, besides, less common except in Maryland and certain parts of Virginia.

The preference given in the West Indies to the staves from Baltimore and Norfolk is due, in a great measure, to their being made of the Post Oak.

This tree, though only of secondary size, should be propagated in America and introduced into the forests of Europe.

PLATE V.

A branch with leaves and fruit of the natural size.

OVER-CUP OAK.

QUERCUS LYRATA. *Q. foliis subsessilibus, glabris, lyrato-sinuosis, summitate dilatatâ, divaricato-trilobâ, lobis acutangulis, terminali tricuspide; cupulâ depresso-globosâ, muricato scabratâ; glande subtectâ.*

In the United States I have met with this interesting species only in the lower part of the Carolinas and of Georgia. It probably exists on the banks of the Mississippi in Lower Louisiana, and I have observed it on the St. John in East Florida, in situations analogous to those in which it flourishes a little farther north. In Georgia and Carolina it is not extensively multiplied, and has been distinguished only by the inhabitants of the places where it grows. It is called Swamp Post Oak, Over-cup Oak, and Water White Oak. The first of these denominations indicates an analogy between its foliage and that of the Post Oak, and the second, a remarkable peculiarity of its fruit, of which the acorn is covered by the cup. The name of Over-cup Oak is the most common in South Carolina, and that of Swamp Post Oak on the Savannah in Georgia.

The Over-cup Oak grows in more humid situations than any other species of this genus in the United States. It is never seen in the long narrow marshes which intersect the pine-barrens, but is found exclusively in the great swamps on the borders of the rivers, which are often overflowed at the rising of the waters, and are inaccessible during three quarters of the year. In these gloomy forests it is united with the Large Tupelo, White Elm, Wahoo, Planer Tree, Carolinian Poplar, Water Bitternut Hickory and Water Locust.

It expands to a majestic size, and the influence of a deep and constantly humid soil is shown in the luxuriancy of its vegetation. On the banks of the Savannah I have seen stocks which were more than 80 feet high and from 8 to 12 feet in circumference. The leaves are 6 or 8 inches long, smooth, narrow, lyre-shaped, deeply sinuated, and borne by short petioles. The lobes, particularly the two upper ones, are truncated, and from their resemblance in this respect to those of the Post Oak, is derived the name of Swamp Post Oak. The foliage is thick and of a light agreeable tint. The acorns, unlike those of the Oaks in general which are of an elongated oval shape, are broad, round, and depressed at the summit : they are sometimes from 12 to 18 lines in diameter from side to side, and from 6 to 10 lines from the base to the summit. The cup, which is nearly closed, is thin, and its scales are terminated by short firm points.

The bark upon the trunk is white, and the wood, though inferior to that of the White Oak and the Post Oak, is more compact than would be supposed from the soil in which it grows; the pores are observable only between the concentrical circles, and are more regularly disposed than in other trees.

This species is the largest and the most highly esteemed among the Oaks that grow in wet grounds. Its propagation should be attempted in the forests of Europe, where no doubt can be entertained of its success. The acorns which I sent to France several years since, though sown upon uplands, have produced flourishing plants, which bear the winter of Paris without injury.

PLATE VI.

A branch with leaves and fruit of the natural size.

Over Cup Oak.

Quercus lyrata.

SWAMP WHITE OAK.

QUERCUS PRINUS DISCOLOR. *Q. foliis oblongo - obovatis,*
subtus albo-tomentosis, grosse dentatis, basi integerrimis,
dentibus inæqualibus dilatatis; fructibus longe pedun-
culatis.

Quercus bicolor. WILLD.

THIS species is known in the United States only by
the name of Swamp White Oak, which indicates at
once the soil which it prefers and its analogy to the
White Oak.

I first observed it near Portsmouth in New Hampshire ; but it is less multiplied in this latitude than in
the Middle and Western States. It particularly attracted
my attention in New Jersey near the city of New York,
on the Delaware in Pennsylvania, on the Susquehannah in Virginia, and beyond the mountains on the
Ohio in Kentucky and on the Holston near Knoxville in
East Tennessee; I have also seen it on the shores of
lake Champlain and lake Ontario. Except the District of
Maine and the maritime parts of the Southern *Section*,
it is diffused throughout the United States ; in comparison, however, with several other species, it is not common, being found only on the edges of swamps and
in wet places exposed to inundations, and not in the
forests at large, like the White Oak, the Black Oak, etc.
In New Jersey it is associated with the Pin Oak, the Red-

flowering Maple, the White Ash, the Tupelo and the Shell-bark Hickory. On the shores of Lake Champlain, which occasionally offer similar situations, particularly at a little distance from Skeensborough, it is mingled with the White Maples, which occupy the next line to the Willows in retiring from the shore.

The Swamp White Oak is a beautiful tree, more than 70 feet in height, of which the vegetation is vigorous and the foliage luxuriant. The leaves are 6 or 8 inches long and 4 inches broad, smooth and of a dark green above, downy and lighter coloured beneath; they are entire towards the base, which is cuneiform, but are widened and coarsely toothed for two thirds of their length towards the summit. The tree is distinguished; when young, by the form of its base and by the down upon its leaves, which is more sensible to the touch than on any analogous species. At a riper age the lower side of the leaf is of a silvery white, which is strikingly contrasted with the bright green of the upper surface; hence the specific name of *discolor* was given it by Dr. Muhlemberg.

The acorns are sweet, but seldom abundant; they are rather large, of a brown complexion, and contained in a spreading cup edged with short slender filaments, more downy within than those of any other Oak, and supported by peduncles 1 or 2 inches in length.

The trunk is clad in a scaly greyish white bark. The wood is strong, elastic, and heavier than that of the

Swamp White Oak
Quercus P.us discolor .

White Oak. In stocks more than a foot in diameter the grain is fine and close, and the pores are nearly obliterated. It splits easily and in a straight line, and is esteemed next in quality to the White Oak, though from its rareness it is but accidentally employed in the arts.

If, as I incline to believe, the Swamp White Oak is found by more accurate experiments to be superior to the White Oak, it must be considered as a very valuable tree, and its increase should be favoured at the expense of the Red-flowering Maple, the Bitternut Hickory, the Hornbeam, and other species which grow in the same exposures. It seems also to deserve a place in the forests of Europe, where, in moist grounds, it might be blended or alternated with the Ashes, the Alders and the Poplars.

PLATE VII.

A branch with leaves and fruit of the natural size.

CHESNUT WHITE OAK.

QUERCUS PRINUS PALUSTRIS. *Q. foliis oblongo-ovalibus, acuminatis acutisve, subuniformiter dentatis; cupulâ crateratâ, subsquamosâ; glande ovatâ.*

Quercus prinus. WILLD.

THE Chesnut White Oak is first seen within ten miles of Philadelphia; but it is less multiplied and less amply developed than farther south. It is most abundant in the maritime parts of the Carolinas, Georgia and East Florida, and is probably found on the banks of the Mississippi, which are analogous to those of many rivers of the Southern States.

In Pennsylvania this species is confounded with the Rock Chesnut Oak, which it strikingly resembles; farther South, where the Rock Chesnut Oak is unknown, it is called Chesnut White Oak, Swamp Chesnut Oak, and generally on the Savannah White Oak.

The Chesnut White Oak is adorned with beautiful foliage : the leaves are 8 or 9 inches long, 4 or 5 inches broad, obovate, deeply toothed, of a light shining green above and whitish beneath.

The acorns are brown, oval, larger than those of any other species except the Over-cup White Oak, and contained in shallow scaly cups. Being sweet-flavoured, and sometimes abundant, they are sought with avidity by wild and domestic animals, such as deer, cows, horses and swine.

The Chesnut White Oak, like the. Over-cup Oak, grows only in the large swamps that border the rivers or are enclosed in the forests; but it always chooses spots that are rarely inundated, where the soil is loose, deep, constantly cool and luxuriantly fertile.

In the Carolinas and Georgia it is usually accompanied by the White Elm, the Wahoo, the Big Laurel, the Umbrella Tree, the Sweet Leaves, the Beech, the Poplar, the Bitternut Hickory and the Devil Wood. In this latitude it attains its utmost developement, which is 80 or 90 feet in stature with a proportional diameter. Its straight trunk, undivided and of an uniform size to the height of 50 feet, and its expansive tufted summit, form one of the most beautiful and majestic trees of the North American forests.

Its wood, which is affected by the richness of the soil, is inferior to that of the Post Oak, the White Oak, and even the Over-cup Oak; and its pores, though nearly obliterated, are more open. But it is superior to many other species, and is employed for wheel-wrights' works and for other objects which require strength and durability. As it splits in a straight line, and may be divided into fine shreds, it is chosen by the negroes for baskets and brooms. Its pores are too open to contain wine or spirituous liquors. In the form of rails it lasts 12 or 15 years, or a third longer than the

Willow Oak. At Augusta in Georgia it is considered as the best fuel, and is sold at 2 or 3 dollars a cord.

The Chesnut White Oak endures the winter of Paris, but its vegetation would be quicker in the more southern departments. It is to be regretted that a tree which seems formed to be one of the finest ornaments of our forests, should have nothing to recommend it but its beauty. Other properties it possesses only in a secondary degree, and in Europe it will probably be confined to the pleasure-grounds of amateurs.

PLATE VIII.

A branch with leaves and fruit of the natural size.

Pl. 8.

Chesnut White Oak.

Quercus P.^{us} palustris.

ROCK CHESNUT OAK.

QUERCUS PRINUS MONTICOLA. *Q. foliis obovatis acutis, grosse dentatis, dentibus subæqualibus; fructu majusculo, cupulâ turbinatâ, scabrosâ; glande oblongâ.*

Quercus montana, WILLD.

THIS Oak is among the species which are not scattered promiscuously in the forests, but which grow only in particular situations and easily escape observation; hence it is difficult to assign its limits with precision. It probably does not extend northward far beyond Vermont, nor eastward beyond New Hampshire. I have never seen it in the District of Maine nor in Nova Scotia, and it is not mentioned in my father's botanical notes upon Lower Canada; it is likewise a stranger to the maritime parts of the Southern States. It is most frequently met with in the Middle and in some parts of the Northern *Sections*; but is rarely mingled with other trees in the forests, and is found only on high grounds thickly strewed with stones or covered with rocks. Thus it is often seen on the steep and rocky banks of the Hudson and on the shores of Lake Champlain, and still more frequently on the Alleghanies in Pennsylvania and Virginia. It forms nine tenths of the growth on some parts of these mountains, but the soil is so meager that it is thinly disseminated

I. 7

and does not exceed 20 or 25 feet in height and 8 or 10 inches in diameter. I made this observation particularly on the *Dry Ridges* 15 miles from Bedford.

In that part of Pennsylvania, as well as in Maryland and Virginia, it is known by the name of Chesnut Oak, and by that of Rock Oak on the banks of the Hudson and the shores of Lake Champlain to the distance of 400 miles from New York. Both are significant; the first, of a remarkable resemblance of the bark to that of the Chesnut; and the second, of the situations in which the tree is exclusively found. For this reason, and to avoid confounding it with the preceding and following species, which also grow in Virginia, I have blended the two denominations.

The beautiful appearance of this tree when growing in a fertile soil, is owing equally to the symmetry of its form and to the luxuriance of its foliage. The leaves are 5 or 6 inches long, 3 or 4 broad, oval and uniformly denticulated, with the teeth more regular but less acute than those of the Chesnut White Oak. When beginning to open in the spring, they are covered with a thick down; but, when fully expanded, they are perfectly smooth, whitish beneath, and of a delicate texture. The petiole is of a yellow colour, which becomes brighter towards the fall.

The acorns are brown, of an oblong-oval shape, and sometimes an inch in length, a third part of which is contained in a spreading cup covered with loose scales:

they are sweet-tasted and are a favourite nourishment of wild and domestic animals.

The Rock Chesnut Oak is sometimes 3 feet in diameter, and more than 60 feet high; but as its growth is usually repressed by the poverty of the soil, it rarely attains these dimensions. In open elevated situations it spreads widely, and forms a head like that of the Apple Tree. When the trunk exceeds a foot in diameter it is covered with a thick, hard, deeply furrowed bark. At New York and near the Alleghanies in Pennsylvania, this species of bark is esteemed the best for tanning. Only that of the secondary branches and of stocks less than 6 inches thick is employed. It is sold at New York for 10 or 12 dollars a cord. The epidermis is strongly impregnated with the tanning principle, which in other species resides only in the cellular integument.

The wood is reddish like that of the White Oak, but its pores are more open, though its specific gravity is greater : pieces of both species being thrown into water, the White Oak remains on the surface and the other at the bottom. Its staves are not used to contain spirituous liquors. At New York and on the banks of the Hudson, it holds the next place to the White Oak in the construction of vessels. It is employed for the lower part of the frame, and oftener for the knees and the ribs : pieces of White Oak suited to these objects are procured with difficulty; but the Rock Chesnut Oak, growing up in a continual controversy with the winds, is more frequently bent into the proper shape. For fuel, it is next in price to the Hickory. I have been told in several forges, especially those at the foot of the *North Mountain*, 200 miles from Philadelphia, that it is superior in this respect to every other species of its genus except the Live Oak.

A tree like this, which grows in stony soils, in abrupt uninhabitable exposures, and whose bark and timber are so valuable, deserves the particular attention of American and European foresters. They should sow the acorns in the crevices of the rocks, and wherever the soil is incapable of cultivation. Thousands of young plants already exist in the vicinity of Paris.

PLATE IX.

A branch with leaves and fruit of the natural size.

Pl 9

Rock Chesnut Oak.

Quercus P.us monticola

YELLOW OAK.

QUERCUS PRINUS ACUMINATA. *Q. foliis longè petiolatis, acuminatis, subæqualiter dentatis; fructu mediocri; cupulâ subhemisphericâ.*

Quercus castanea, WILLD.

THE banks of the Delaware may be assumed as the northern limit of the Yellow Oak. It scarcely exists in the maritime parts of the Southern States, where I have seen only a few stocks near Two Sisters' Ferry on the Savannah in Georgia, and a single one on the Cape Fear, a mile from Fayetteville in North Carolina. In the Middle and Western States, though more common, it is still rare in comparison with many other trees, and is sometimes lost sight of by the traveller for several days in succession. I have most particularly observed it on the small river Conestoga near Lancaster in Pennsylvania, on the Mononghahela a little above Pittsburgh, and in several small tracts near the Holston and Nolachuky in East Tennessee. In the Monography of American Oaks, my father takes notice of its existence in the country of the Illinois.

Near Lancaster this tree is called Yellow Oak, from the complexion of its wood; but in other parts of the United States it is confounded with the Chesnut White Oak and Rock Chesnut Oak, to which it bears some resemblance in its foliage.

The leaves are lanceolate, regularly toothed, of a light green above and whitish beneath. The small acorns are contained in slightly scaly cups, and are sweeter than those of any other species in the United States.

The Yellow Oak is a fine tree, 70 or 80 feet high and 2 feet in diameter, with branches tending rather to close round the trunk than to diffuse themselves horizontally. I invariably found it in vallies where the soil was loose, deep and fertile. The bark upon the trunk is whitish, very slightly furrowed, and sometimes divided into plates, like that of the Swamp White Oak. The wood is yellowish, though the tint is not bright enough to fit it for peculiar uses. Its pores are partly obliterated, irregularly disposed, and more numerous than those of any other American Oak : this organisation must impair its strength and render it less durable than the Chesnut White Oak and the Rock Chesnut Oak.

As this tree is so thinly disseminated, it will not appear surprising that I should not have witnessed the application of its wood in the arts, or have found occasions of accurately appreciating its qualities. Its agreeable form and beautiful foliage render it proper for the embellishment of picturesque gardens.

PLATE X.

A branch with leaves and fruit of the natural size.

Yellow Oak.

Quercus P.ᵘˢ acuminata.

SMALL CHESNUT OAK.

QUERCUS PRINUS CHINCAPIN. *Q. foliis obovatis, grosse dentatis, subtus glaucis; cupulâ hemisphæricâ; glande ovatâ.*

Quercus prinoides, WILLD.

IN the Northern and Middle States this pretty little species is called Small or Dwarf Chesnut Oak, from the resemblance of its leaves to those of the Rock Chesnut Oak; as there is also a likeness between its foliage and that of the Chincapin, it is known in East Tennessee and in the upper part of the Carolinas by the name of Chincapin Oak.

The Small Chesnut Oak is not generally diffused, but is rare in many places adapted to its constitution, and is usually found in particular districts, where, alone or mingled with the Bear Oak, it sometimes covers tracts of more than 100 acres. The presence of these species is a certain proof of the barrenness of the soil. I have particularly observed the Small Chesnut Oak in the vicinity of Providence in Rhode Island, of Albany in New York, of Knoxville in Tennessee, and on the Alleghany Mountains in Virginia. It grows spontaneously in the park of Mr. W. Hamilton near Philadelphia.

This species and another which is found in the Pine forests of the Southern States rarely exceed 3o inches in height : they are the most diminutive of the American Oaks, and are mentioned only to complete the series.

The leaves of the Small Chesnut Oak are oval-acuminate, regularly but not deeply denticulated , of a light
green above and whitish beneath. The acorns are enclosed for one third of their length in scaly sessile cups ;
they are of a middle size, sowewhat elongated, similarly
rounded at both ends, and very sweet.

Nature seems to have sought a compensation for the
diminutive size of this shrub in the abundance of its
fruit : the stem, which is sometimes no bigger than a
quill, is stretched at full length upon the ground by the
weight of the thickly clustering acorns. United with the
Bear Oak, which is of the same size and equally prolific,
perhaps it might be cultivated with advantage for its
fruit.

PLATE XI.

A branch with leaves and fruit of the natural size.

Pl. 11.

Small Chesnut Oak.

Quercus P. chincapin.

LIVE OAK.

Quercus virens. *Q. foliis perennantibus, coriaceis, ovato-oblongis, junioribus dentatis, vetustioribus integris; cupulâ turbinatâ, squamulis abbreviatis; glande oblongâ.*

This species, which is confined to the maritime parts of the Southern States, the Floridas and Louisiana, is known only by the name of Live Oak. The climate becomes mild enough for its growth near Norfolk in Virginia, though it is less multiplied and less vigorous than in a more southern latitude. From Norfolk it spreads along the coast for a distance of 15 or 18 hundred miles, extending beyond the mouth of the Mississippi. The sea-air seems essential to its existence, for it is rarely found in the forests upon the mainland, and never more than 15 or 20 miles from the shore.

It is the most abundant, the most fully developed, and of the best quality, about the bays and creeks, and on the fertile islands which in great numbers lie scattered for several hundred miles along the coast. I particularly observed it on the islands of St. Simon, Cumberland, Sapelo, etc., between the St. John and the St. Mary, in an excursion of four or five hundred miles in a canoe, from Cape Canaveral in East Florida to Savannah in Georgia. I frequently saw it upon the beach, or half-buried in the moveable sands upon the downs, where it had preserved its freshness and vigour, though exposed during a long lapse of time to the fury of the wintry tempest and to the ardour of the summer's sun.

The Live Oak is commonly 40 or 45 feet in height, and from 1 to 2 feet in diameter; but it is sometimes much larger : Mr. S., president of the Agricultural Society of Charleston, assured me that he had felled a trunk, hollowed by age, which was 24 feet in circumference. Like most other trees, it has, when insulated, a wide and tufted summit. Its trunk is sometimes undivided for 18 or 20 feet, but often ramifies at half this height, and at a distance it has the appearance of an old Apple Tree or Pear Tree. The leaves are oval, coriaceous, of a dark green above and whitish beneath : they persist during several years, and are partially renewed every spring. On trees reared upon plantations, or growing in cool soils, they are one half larger, and are often denticulated : upon stocks of two or three years they are commonly very distinctly toothed.

The acorns are of a lengthened oval form, nearly black, and contained in shallow, greyish, pedunculated cups. The Indians are said to have expressed an oil from them to mingle with their food; perhaps, also, they eat the kernel, which, though not agreeable to the taste, is less rough and bitter than that of many other species. The fruit is sometimes very abundant, and it germinates with such ease that if the weather is rainy at the season of its maturity, many acorns are found upon the trees with the radicle unfolded.

The bark upon the trunk is blackish, hard and thick. The wood is heavy, compact, fine-grained, and of a yellowish colour, which deepens as the tree advances in age. The number and closeness of the concentrical circles evince the slowness of its growth. As it is very strong, and incomparably more durable than the best White Oak, it is highly esteemed in ship-building, and is consumed not only in the country which produces it, but still more extensively in the Northern States. From its great durability when perfectly seasoned it is almost exclusively employed for the upper part of the frame. To compensate its excessive weight it is joined with the Red Cedar, which is extremely light and equally lasting.

The Live Oak does not afford large timber; but its wide and branching summit makes amends for this disadvantage by furnishing a great number of knees, of which there is never a sufficient quantity in the dockyards.

The vessels built at New York and Philadelphia, with the upper frame of Red Cedar and Live Oak, and the lower timbers of White Oak, are as durable as those constructed of the best materials in Europe. Brekel, whom I have already quoted, says that the best trunnels are of Live Oak ; but at present it is replaced, in the Southern States, by the Locust and the heart of the Long-leaved Pine.

In the South, particularly at Charleston and Savannah, this species is used for the naves and felloes of heavy wheels, for which it is far superior to the White Oak : it is more proper, also, for screws and for the cogs of mill-wheels.

The bark is excellent for tanning, but is only accidentally employed.

Besides the Live Oak timber exported to England, great quantities are used in ship-building in the United States, particularly at Boston, New York, Philadelphia and Baltimore. The consumption has become threefold within twenty years, in consequence of the immense developement of American commerce. Hence the price has doubled, and the species is rapidly diminishing. The clearing of the islands for the culture of cotton, which they yield of a superior quality, has contributed greatly to its destruction. It is already difficult to procure sticks of considerable size in the Southern States, and they are sought on the western coast of East Florida between the St. Mary and the St. John. From St. Augustine to the Cape the species is rarer ; but we are informed that it abounds on the shores of West Florida, whither the English of the Bahama Islands resort for supplies.

As the Live Oak, from the peculiarities of its constitution, is multiplied with difficulty, I cannot but consider its disappearance throughout the United States within fifty years as nearly certain. It will then be

Live Oak.

Quercus virens.

found only in the form of a shrub, like the *Quercus ilex* which formerly skirted the southern coast of France and Italy.

PLATE XII.

A branch with leaves and fruit of the natural size.

CORK OAK.

QUERCUS SUBER. *Q. foliis ovato-oblongis, indivisis, serratis, subtus glaucis; cortice rimoso, fungoso.*

THE Cork Oak grows naturally in the southern parts of France, in Spain, Portugal, Italy and the States of Barbary, which are comprised between the 44th and 35th degrees of latitude. It rarely exceeds 40 feet in height and 3 feet in diameter. Its leaves are evergreen, but the greater part of them fall and are renewed in the spring: they are ovate, thick, slightly toothed, of a light green on the upper surface and glaucous beneath. The acorns are rather large, oval, and half enclosed in a conical cup: as they are of a sweetish taste, they are eagerly devoured by swine.

The wood is hard, compact and heavy, but less durable than that of the Common European Oak, particularly when exposed to humidity. The worth of the tree resides in its bark, which begins to be taken off at the age of 25 years. The first growth is of little value; in ten years it is renewed; but the second product, though less cracked than the first, is not thick enough for corks, and is used only by fishermen to buoy up their nets. It is not till the tree is 45 or 50 years old that the bark possesses all the qualities requisite for good corks, and from that period it is collected once in eight or ten years. Its thickness is owing to the extraordinary swelling of the cellular integument. It is better fitted than any other substance for the use to which it is appropriated, as its elasticity exactly adapts it to the neck of the bottle, and its impenetrable structure refuses admission to the fluid.

July and August are the seasons for gathering it. For this purpose two opposite longitudinal incisions are made through the whole length of the trunk, and two others, transverse to the first, at the extremities; the bark is then detached by inserting a hatchet-handle shaped like a wedge. Great care must be taken not to wound the alburnum, as the bark is never renewed upon the injured parts. After being scraped, the bark is heated on its convex side, and laden with stones, to flatten it and render it easier of transportation. In Catalonia it is cut into pieces and boiled to improve its quality. Its excellence consists in being compact, supple and elastic and it should be from 15 to 20 lines thick.

The cork produced in France may be reckoned at 17 or 18,000 quintals, and when the sheets are smooth and even each quintal affords 7,000 or 7,500 corks 18 lines long. The common price is a dollar and 70 cents a thousand, of which 50 cents must be allowed for the expense of making. It is computed that 110 or 115 millions of corks are annually consumed in France.

This tree would be an important acquisition to the United States, and would grow wherever the Live Oak

subsists. The soil of-the *pine barrens* is in general too
meager to sustain its vegetation; the bed of vegetable
mould is in many places so thin, and the sand beneath
so homogeneous, that the roots of the Pines, instead
of shooting downward, fold themselves back, as if re-
pelled by a solid rock.

Both public and private interest requires the inhabitants of the Southern coast, and especially of the neighbouring islands, to rear the Cork Oak about their plantations and in places that are unfit for the cultivation of
cotton. It should also be introduced into West Tennessee, and with the more reason as the Vine may be cultivated there with success.

As the young stocks are injured by transplanting,
they should be permanently fixed the second or third
year. To favour their growth, the earth should be loos-
ened about the roots two or three times a year; and to
render them tall and well-shaped, the lower branches
should be cut even with the trunk. Their vegetation is
in this manner strengthened and the bark improved;
without farther attention they will continue to afford a
valuable product during two or three centuries.

This tree has great advantages over several others
which would likewise flourish in the same parts of the
United States, such as the Olive and the White Mulberry. To fit their produce for consumption, particularly that of the Mulberry, requires complicated proces-
ses, which can be performed with advantage only in

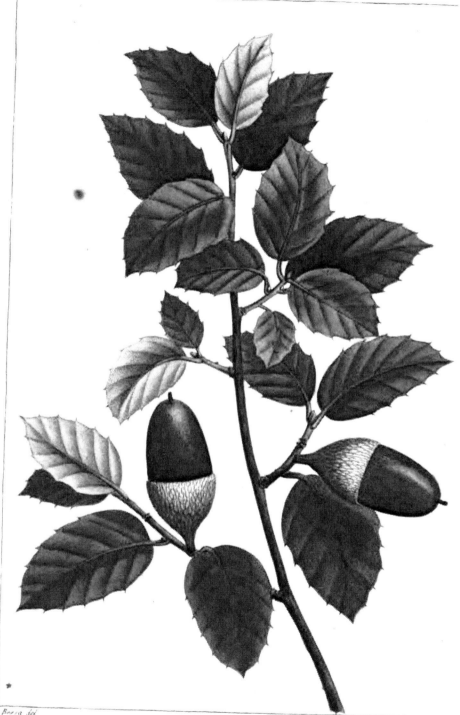

Cork Oak.
Quercus suber.

populous countries. Hence the attempts made 70 or 80 years ago in Georgia to introduce the rearing of silk-worms proved abortive; and the old White Mulberry Trees that still remain are monuments of that ill-calculated speculation. The bark of the Cork Oak, on the contrary, might be transported to the Northern States, or made into corks upon the spot by a simple operation performed by a single person with instruments of which the price does not exceed two or three dollars.

PLATE XIII.

A branch with leaves and fruit of the natural size.

WILLOW OAK.

QUERCUS PHELLOS. *Q. foliis lineari-lanceolatis, integerrimis, glabris, apice setaceo-acuminatis, junioribus dentatis lobatisve; cupulâ scutellatâ; glande subrotundâ, minimâ.*

THIS species, which is remarkable for its foliage, makes its first appearance in the environs of Philadelphia; but it is more common and of a larger size in Virginia, the Carolinas and Georgia, where the milder temperature of the winter is evidently favourable to its growth. It is seen, however, only in the maritime parts of those States, and is a stranger to the inland districts, where the surface is mountainous and the climate more severe. From the analogy of soil and climate it is probably found in Lower Louisiana, but I have never observed it beyond the Alleghanies in Kentucky and Tennessee.

The Willow Oak commonly grows in cool moist places, and, with the Tupelo, the Small Magnolia, the Red-flowering Maple, the Red Bay and the Water Oak, it borders the swamps in the lower part of the Southern States. In these situations it attains its greatest expansion, which is 5o or 6o feet in height and from 2o to 24 inches in diameter. The trunk, even at an advanced age, is covered with a smooth bark, remarkable for the thickness of its cellular integument. The leaves are 2 or 3 inches long, of a light green, smooth, narrow, entire, and similar to those of the Willow, whence is derived the name of Willow Oak, which is used in every part of North America where the tree is known.

Though the Willow Oak, as I have just observed, is almost always seen in moist grounds, by an exception for which it is difficult to account it is sometimes found among the Live Oaks, near the sea, in the driest and most sandy soils. At a distance it resembles the Live Oak in its shape, and in its foliage which persists during several years; but on a closer examination it is easily distinguished by the form of its leaves, which are shorter and much narrower, and by the porous texture of its wood.

The fruit of this species is rarely abundant; the acorns are of a dark brown colour, small, round, bitter, and contained in shallow cups lightly coated with scales : kept in a cool place they preserve the faculty of germination for several months.

The wood is reddish and coarse-grained. It is too porous to contain wine or spirituous liquor, and its staves are classed with those of Red Oak. The quantity, however, is small, as the tree is so little multiplied that alone it would not supply the consumption for two years. In some of the lower parts of Virginia, particularly in the county of York, it is found to possess great strength and tenacity, and to split less easily than the White Oak; hence, after being thoroughly seasoned, it is employed for the felloes of wheels. These are the only uses to which it seems adapted, and for these it is less proper than the Post Oak and White Ash. On several plantations near Augusta in Georgia the fences are made partly of Willow Oak, which lasts only eight or nine years. As fuel, it is sold at the lowest price.

PLATE XIV.

A branch with leaves and fruit of the natural size.

Redouté del.

Renard Sc.

Willow Oak.

Quercus phellos.

LAUREL OAK.

QUERCUS IMBRICARIA. *Q. foliis subsessilibus, ovali-oblongis, acutis, integerrimis, nitidis; glande subhemisphœricâ.*

EAST of the Alleghanies this species is rare, and has received no specific name; west of the mountains, where it is more multiplied and has attracted more attention, it is called Jack Oak, Black Jack Oak, and sometimes, from the form of its leaves, Laurel Oak. The last denomination I have preserved as the most appropriate, though perhaps it is less common than the first.

I observed this tree for the first time in Pennsylvania near Bedford on the Juniata, upon the road from Philadelphia to Pittsburgh, and it does not exist in the more Northern States. I found it abundant only beyond the mountains, and particularly near Washington Courthouse and in some parts of Kentucky and Tennessee. From my father's observations it appears to be more multiplied in the country of the Illinois than in the places I have just mentioned, and it is called by the French *Chêne à lattes*, Lath Oak.

In the western parts of Pennsylvania and Virginia, small lawns, covered only with tall grass, are frequently seen in the forests, around which the Laurel Oak forms entire groves : insulated stocks are also found in cool humid situations. It is probably from its flourishing in open exposures that it is most abundant in the country of the Illinois, which consists of immeasurable savannas stretching in every direction, to which the forests bear no sensible proportion.

The Laurel Oak is 40 or 50 feet high, and 12 or 15 inches in diameter. Its trunk, even when old, is clad in a smooth bark, and, for three fourths of its height, is laden with branches. It has an uncouth form when bared in the winter, but is beautiful in the summer when clad in its thick tufted foliage. The leaves are long, lanceolate, entire, and of a light shining green.

The wood is hard and heavy, though its pores are open. As the trunk is branchy and often crooked, it is considered, wherever I have observed it, as fit only for fuel; but my father, who first described it, says that the French of Illinois use it for shingles. Probably in that region it attains much greater dimensions; but in my opinion the want of better species only can account for its use. Its wood is inferior to that of the Willow Oak, which it nearly resembles.

This tree has no merit but its singular foliage, and it deserves the attention only of amateurs desirous of adorning their rural retreats with a variety of exotic trees.

PLATE XV.

A branch with leaves and fruit of the natural size.

Pl.15

Laurel Oak.

Quercus imbricaria.

UPLAND WILLOW OAK.

QUERCUS CINEREA. *Q. foliis petiolatis, lanceolato-oblongis, acutis, integerrimis, subtus cinereo-pubescentibus; cupulâ scutellatâ; glande subhemisphæricâ.*

THE Upland Willow Oak is confined to the maritime parts of the Southern States. It is little multiplied in comparison with many other species, and is dispersed in small groups in the forests of White Pine. It is found also upon the sea-shore, and upon the islands where it covers tracts of several acres still more barren than the main. But the stocks which grow in these different situations are so different in appearance that they might easily be mistaken for distinct species : in the *pine-barrens* they are 18 or 20 feet high, and 4 or 5 inches in diameter, with the leaves entire, 2 inches and a half long, and whitish underneath; on the islands and on the shore of the Continent, where the soil is extremely dry, as near Wilmington, N. C., they are only 3 or 4 feet in height, and the leaves are denticulated, are an inch in length, and persist for two years. I have ascertained that both varieties belong to the same species, by examining the sprouts of the larger stocks in the *pine-barrens*, of which the foliage is perfectly similar to that of the smaller ones on the shore.

The Upland Willow Oak is one of the abject trees

that succeed the Pines on lands which have been cleared for cultivation and abandoned on account of their sterility. In these places, as in the *pine-barrens*, it is 20 feet in stature, and its trunk, crooked and covered with a thick bark, begins at a third of this height to divide itself by numerous ramifications. In the spring it is distinguished at a distance by the reddish colour of its leaves and male aments. The acorns, which are contained in shallow cups, are round and blackish, with the base of a bright rose colour when freshly exposed. It is rare to meet with a tree which yields a quart of fruit.

The bark of this species, like that of the Black Oak, affords a beautiful yellow dye; but the tree is so small and so little multiplied that it is of no utility in this respect, nor even for fuel.

The *Quercus nana* of Willdenow is certainly the smaller variety of this species.

PLATE XVI.

A branch with leaves and fruit of the natural size. Fig. 1, A leaf of the smaller variety of the natural size.

Upland Willow Oak
Quercus cinerea.

RUNNING OAK.

QUERCUS PUMILA. *Q. foliis deciduis, lanceolatis, integer-rimis, basi attenuatis, apice dilatatis; cupulâ scutellatâ; glande subhemisphæricâ.*

Quercus sericea, WILLD.

THIS species, which is rarely more than 20 inches in height and 2 lines in diameter, is the smallest Oak hitherto discovered in the Old or the New World. Like the Upland Willow Oak, it is confined to the maritime parts of the Carolinas, Georgia and the Floridas, where it is called Running Oak. It springs with that species in the *pine-barrens,* amid the numerous varieties of Whortleberry and other plants which overspread the ground wherever there is a little moisture in the soil and the layer of vegetable mould is a few inches thick.

The leaves of this dwarfish shrub are of a reddish tint in the spring, and turn green as the season advances. When fully developed they are entire, smooth, of an elongated oval shape, and about 2 inches in length. The acorns are small, round, and similar to those of the Willow and Water Oaks : they are few in number, because the stem is burnt to the surface of the ground almost every spring, by the fire which is kindled in the forests to consume the dead grass ; as this species belongs to the division whose fructification

is biennial, the acorns are destroyed before they arrive
at maturity.

My own observations, and those of Messrs. Bosc and
Delille, distinguished botanists who resided several years
in the Southern part of the United States, have led me
to consider the Running Oak as a distinct species and
not as a variety of the Willow Oak, as my father has
treated it in his *monography* of this important genus. It
is hardly necessary to remark that from its size it can
be interesting only to botanists.

PLATE. XVII.

A branch with leaves and fruit of the natural size.

Pl. 17.

Running Oak.
Quercus pumila.

BARTRAM OAK.

QUERCUS HETEROPHYLLA. *Q. foliis longe petiolatis, ovato-lanceolatis, integris vel inæqualiter dentatis; glande sub-globosâ.*

EVERY botanist who has visited different regions of the globe must have remarked certain species of vegetables which are so little multiplied that they seem likely at no distant period to disappear from the earth. To this class belongs the Bartram Oak. Several English and American naturalists who, like my father and myself, have spent years in exploring the United States, and who have obligingly communicated to us the result of their observations, have, like us, found no traces of this species except a single stock in a field belonging to Mr. Bartram, on the banks of the Schuylkill, 4 miles from Philadelphia. This is a flourishing tree, 3o feet in height and 12 inches in diameter, and seems formed to attain a much greater developement. Its leaves are of an elongated oval form, coarsely and irregularly toothed, smooth above, and of a dark green beneath. The acorns are round, of a middle size, and contained in shallow cups lightly covered with scales.

I was at first disposed to consider this tree as a variety of the Laurel Oak, to which it bears the greatest affinity; but the leaves of that species are never indented, and not a stock of it exists within a hundred miles of Philadelphia.

Several young plants, which I received from Mr. Bartram himself, have been placed in our public gardens to insure the preservation of the species.

PLATE XVIII.

A branch with leaves and fruit of the natural size.

Pl. 18.

Bartram's Oak.
Quercus heterophilla.

WATER OAK.

QUERCUS AQUATICA. Q. foliis obovali-cuneatis, basi acutis, summitate subintegris, variée trilobis, glabris; cupulá modice crateratá; glande subglobosá.

THIS species first attracted my attention in the forests near Richmond in Virginia; it becomes more common in proceeding southward, and abounds in the lower part of the Carolinas and Georgia, and in East Florida. Under the name of Water Oak it is sometimes confounded with the Willow Oak, by which it is always accompanied in the ponds and narrow swamps enclosed in the *pine-barrens*. It is inferior in size to the Willow Oak, and rarely exceeds 40 or 45 feet in height and 12 or 18 inches in diameter. On full-grown trees the leaves are smooth, shining, and heart-shaped — or broad and rounded at the summit and terminated in an acute angle at the base. In the severe climate of Virginia they fall with the first frost, but on the sea-shore of the Carolinas, Georgia and Florida, they persist during two or three years. There is no Oak in the United States of which the foliage is so variable and so different from that of the tree, on the young stocks and on the sprouts from an old trunk or from the base of a limb that has been lopped : the leaves are commonly oval and deeply and irregularly toothed.

The acorns, which are contained in shallow, slightly scaly cups, are brown, small, and extremely bitter; the largest tree rarely yields more than five or six quarts. Like those of the Willow Oak, when kept cool they preserve their fecundity for several months.

The bark upon the oldest trunks is smooth and very slightly furrowed; it is little used in tanning, either because it is inferior to that of the Spanish Oak, or because the tree is less abundant.

The wood is very tough, but less durable and less esteemed by carpenters and wheel-wrights than that of the White Oak and Chesnut White Oak.

As this species is destitute of interest, it will probably become extinct like many others which are rapidly diminishing. In France it would flourish only in the southern departments.

PLATE XIX.

A branch with leaves and fruit of the natural size.

Pl. 19.

Water Oak

Quercus aquatica.

BLACK JACK OAK.

QUERCUS FERRUGINEA. *Q. foliis coriaceis, summitate di-latatis, retuso-subtrilobis, basi retusis, subtus rubiginoso-pulverulentis; cupulâ turbinatâ, squamis obtusis, scariosis; glande brevi ovatâ.*

Quercus nigra, WILLD.

I observed this species for the first time in the forests near Allenstown and Cranbury, small towns of New Jersey, about 60 miles east of Philadelphia; but it is smaller and less multiplied in this place than farther south. In New Jersey and Philadelphia it is called *Barrens Oak*, and Black Jack Oak in Maryland and the more Southern States. I have adopted the last of these names only because it is the most generally used, and have changed the specific epithet *nigra*, because the name of Black Oak is appropriated in the United States to the *Quercus tinctoria.*

This species is commonly found upon soils composed of red argillaceous sand mingled with gravel, and so meager as to be totally exhausted by five or six crops, when they are thought worthy of cultivation. Unhappily from Baltimore to the borders of North Carolina, an extent of four or five hundred miles, the greater part of Maryland and Virginia consists of this soil. The whole of this interval, with the exception of the vallies and the swamps with their surrounding acclivities, is covered

with forests impoverished by fire and by the cattle that
subsist in them during a great part of the year. They are
composed principally of Yellow Pine, Post Oak, Black
Jack Oak, Black Oak and Scarlet Oak. In the Carolinas
and Georgia, where the soil gradually improves in retiring from the shore towards the mountains, the same
tree forms a band 15 or 20 miles wide, between the
pine-barrens and the forests of a more generous growth.
In Kentucky and Tennessee the Black Jack Oak is seen
only in the savannas, where it is widely diffused, and
where, preserved by the thickness of its bark and its insulated position, it survives the conflagrations that almost
every year consume the grass; the fire, driven forward
by the wind, has only time to devour its foliage. In the
pine-barrens it grows chiefly on the edges of the *branch-
swamps*, where the soil is a little stronger than is necessary for the Pines. With the Upland Willow Oak and
the Scrub Oak it possesses itself of the pine lands that
have been cleared for cultivation and abandoned on account of their sterility; and in these situations it is
larger than in the forests.

The Black Jack Oak is sometimes 30 feet high and 8 or
10 inches in dameter, but commonly does not exceed
half these dimensions. Its trunk is generally crooked, and
is covered with a very hard, thick and deeply furrowed
bark, of which the epidermis is nearly black, and the
cellular integument of a dull red. The summit is spacious
even in the midst of the woods. The leaves are yellow-

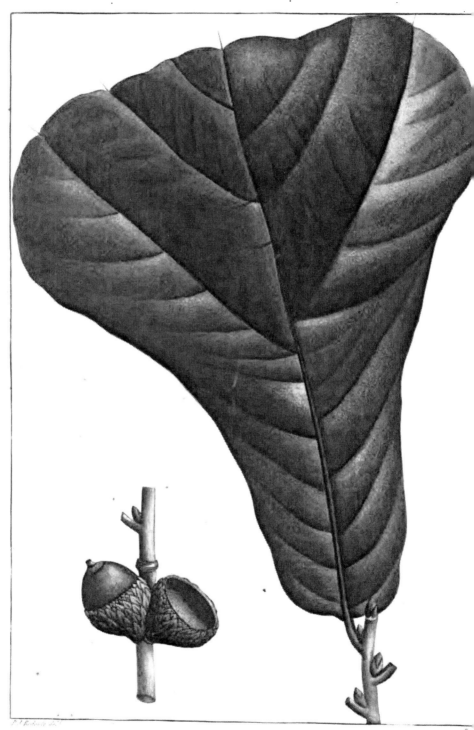

Black Jack Oak.
Quercus ferruginea.

ish, and somewhat downy at their unfolding in the spring; when fully expanded they are of a dark green above, rusty beneath, thick, coriaceous, and dilated towards the summit like a pear. In the autumn they turn reddish, and fall with the earliest frost.

The oldest trees bear only a few handfuls of acorns, which are large, and half covered with very scaly cups.

When the stock is more than 8 inches in diameter, the wood is heavy and compact; but coarse-grained and porous before it has reached this size. As it speedily decays when exposed to the weather, it is not used in the arts. It forms excellent fuel, and is sold at Philadelphia only one dollar a cord less than Hickory, while other kinds of wood are a third cheaper.

This species deserves the attention of amateurs in Europe, for the singularity of its foliage.

PLATE XX.

A branch with leaves and fruit of the natural size.

BEAR OAK.

QUERCUS BANISTERI. *Q. foliis longe petiolatis, acutangulo-quinque-lobis, margine integris, subtus cinereis; cupulâ subturbinatâ; glande subglobosâ.*

THIS diminutive species is known in the Northern and Middle States by the names of Bear Oak, Black Scrub Oak and Dwarf Red Oak, of which the first is the most common in New Jersey, where the shrub abounds. The latin specific name was given it in honour of Banister, an English writer, by whom it was first introduced to notice.

I do not remember to have seen the Bear Oak in the lower part of the Southern States; it is common in those of the North, and still more so, I believe, in New York, New Jersey and Pennsylvania. I have more particularly observed it at Fishkill, Katskill and Albany in New York, near Paramus in New Jersey, and on that part of the Alleghanies in Pennsylvania which is crossed by the road to Pittsburgh. It is never found insulated or mingled with other shrubs in the forests, but always in tracts of several hundred acres, which it covers almost exclusively : a few stocks of the Dwarf Chesnut Oak are often united with it.

The ordinary height of the Bear Oak is 3 or 4 feet ; but when accidentally insulated, and nourished by a vein of more fertile soil, it sometimes equals 8 or 10 feet. It usually grows in compact masses, which are traversed with difficulty, though no higher than the waist. As the individuals which compose them are of an uniform height, they form so even a surface that at a distance the ground appears to be covered with grass instead of shrubs.

The trunk, which is numerously ramified, is covered, like the branches, with a polished bark. It has more strength than would be supposed from its size, which is rarely more than an inch in diameter. The leaves are of a dark green on the upper surface, whitish beneath, and regularly divided into 3 or 5 lobes. The acorns are small, blackish, and longitudinally marked with a few reddish lines : they are so abundant as sometimes to cover the branches ; the lowly stature of the shrub renders it easy for bears, deer and swine to reach them by lifting their heads or rising on their hinder feet.

The presence of this Oak, is considered as an infallible index of a barren soil, and it is usually found on dry sandy land mingled with gravel. It is too small to be adapted to any use ; but near Goshen, on the road to New York, I observed an attempt to turn it to advantage, by planting it about the fields for the purpose of strengthening the fences. Though this experiment seemed to have failed, I believe the Bear Oak might be usefully adopted in the Northern States for hedges, which might be formed from 20 to 24 inches thick, by sowing the

acorns in three parallel furrows. They would be per-
fected in a short time, would be agreeable to the eye,
and probably would be sufficient to prevent the passage
of horses and cows. Hedges of the European Thorn
would doubtless be preferable; but they require a good
soil and more labour than can at present be afforded in
America: those that exist in the neighbourhood of Philadelphia are left in a condition which would give a very
unfavourable opinion of the farmer on whose lands
they were seen in the North of France.

As the Bear Oak grows on the most sterile soils, and
resists the most intense cold and the most impetuous
winds, perhaps it might serve to shelter the infancy of
other more valuable trees in such exposures. The want
of some such protection is the greatest obstacle to the
success of plantations on the downs, as I was told near
the Hague upon the coast of Holland.

Proprietors of large estates, who are addicted to the
chase, might find this species and the Dwarf Chesnut
Oak convenient for copses; they would afford nourishment to the game during several months in the year,
and would allow the sportsman a fair aim at the birds as
they rose upon the wing.

PLATE XXI.

A branch with leaves and fruit of the natural size.

Bear's Oak.

Quercus banisteri.

BARRENS SCRUB OAK.

QUERCUS CATESBÆI. *Q. foliis brevissime petiolatis, sub-palmato-lobatis, lobis interdum subfalcatis; cupulâ ma-jusculâ, squamis marginalibus introflexis; glande brevi ovatâ.*

ACCORDING to my own observations this species is confined to the lower part of the Carolinas and Georgia. I first saw it a few miles south of Raleigh, N. C., latitude 35° 40′. It grows in soils too meager to sustain any other vegetation, such as the vicinity of Wilmington, N. C., where the light moveable sand is wholly destitute of ve-getable mould. It is the only species multiplied in the *pine-barrens,* and from this circumstance it seems to have derived its name.

In traversing these forests I nowhere saw the Scrub Oak more uniformly disseminated than between Fayet-teville and Wilmington, an interval of 60 miles, where it forms nearly one tenth of the woods : the Pines themselves, throughout the barrens, are scattered at the distance of 15 or 20 feet.

The foliage of this tree is open, and its leaves are large, smooth, thick and coriaceous towards the close of summer, deeply and irregularly laciniated, and sup-ported by short petioles. With the first frost they change to a dull red, and fall the ensuing month. The acorns

are pretty large, of a blackish colour, and partly covered
with a fine grey dust, which is easily rubbed off between
the fingers : they are contained in thick cups swollen
towards the edge, with the upper scales bent inwards.
The oldest trees alone are productive, and their fruit
never exceeds a few handfuls.

In the winter it is difficult to distinguish the Scrub
Oak from the Black Jack Oak, which it nearly resembles.
Like that, it is crooked, ramified at the height of 2 or
3 feet, and covered with a thick, blackish, deeply furrowed bark : it is, besides, perfectly similar in the colour, texture and weight of its wood. At Wilmington the
Scrub Oak is the best fuel, and is sold separately; but
notwithstanding its abundance in this district it is insuf-
ficient for the supply of the inhabitants : its size alone
would exclude it from use in the arts.

The general character of this tree forbids the hopes
of advantage that might be conceived from its flourishing upon the most sterile soils.

PLATE XXII.

A branch with leaves and fruit of the natural size.

Barrens Scrub Oak.

Quercus catesbæi.

SPANISH OAK.

QUERCUS FALCATA. *Q. foliis longe petiolatis, subpalmato-lobatis, subtus eximie tomentosis, lobis falcatis; cupulâ crateriformi; glande subglobosâ.*

Quercus elongata, WILLD.

THIS species, like the Black Jack Oak, begins to show itself in New Jersey, near Allentown, about 60 miles from Philadelphia. But even at this distance it is smaller than in the immediate vicinity of the city, where it acquires its perfect developement, and where its leaves exhibit their appropriate form. Farther south it is constantly found among the most common trees in the forests. I have observed that it is less multiplied near the mountains, and in the country beyond them. In Delaware, Maryland and Virginia, it is known only by the name of Spanish Oak, and in the Carolinas and Georgia by that of Red Oak. In an old English work which I found in the library of Charleston, it is said to have been called Spanish Oak by the first settlers, from the resemblance of its leaves to those of the *Quercus velani* which grows in Spain. Whether this etymology is just or not, I am unable to say; but it is unknown to the inhabitants who have adopted the name. The denomination of Red Oak, which is used only in the more Southern States, was probably given it on account of the great analogy between its wood and that of the spe-

cies thus called in the Northern and Middle States,
where the Spanish Oak is much less common than in
the South.

This tree is more than 80 feet in height, and 4 or 5
feet in diameter. Its leaves are very different on different
individuals ; thus in New Jersey, where the tree is only
3o feet high and 4 or 5 inches thick, they are three-
lobed, except a few on the summit, and not falcated
as on the large stocks in the Southern States. On young
plants, and on the lower branches of the most vigorous
stocks growing in moist and shaded situations, they are
also trilobed ; and on the upper limbs they are more
acutely laciniated, with the sections more arching than
those represented in the figure. This remarkable difference led my father to describe as a distinct species,
under the name of *Quercus triloba,* the individuals whose
foliage had not acquired its perfect form. Sometimes,
on the sprouts of trees that have been felled, the leaves
are deeply denticulated at right angles to the main rib.
One of their constant characters is a thick down upon
the lower side of the leaf and upon the young shoots to
which they are attached.

The acorns are small, round, of a brown colour, and
contained in slightly scaly shallow cups supported by
peduncles one or two lines in length. They resemble
those of the Bear Oak, and, like them, preserve for a
long time the faculty of germination.

The bark upon the trunk is blackish and deeply fur-

rowed, with a cellular integument of middling thickness.
The wood is reddish and coarse-grained, with empty
pores, and all the characteristic properties of the species
known in commerce by the general name of Red Oak :
hence its staves are fit only to contain melasses, salted
provisions and dry goods. I have been told that in the
West Indies the Red Oak staves from the Southern
States, where this species abounds, are the most esteemed, from which it seems probable that its wood is
better than that of the Red, Scarlet and Black Oaks that
furnish almost all the Red Oak staves from the Northern
and Middle States : this superiority, however, is not
sufficiently marked to occasion a difference in the price.

From its want of durability the Spanish Oak is less
esteemed than the White Oak, the Post Oak, and other
species of annual fructification. It is rarely employed in
building, and is used by cart-wrights only at Baltimore,
where it is preferred to the White Oak for the felloes
of large wheels.

The principal merit of the Spanish Oak, which gives
it a superiority over most other species of the United
States, resides in its bark. This is preferred for tanning
coarse leather, which it renders whiter and more supple; it is consequently sold at Philadelphia and Wilmington a fourth dearer than that of the other Oaks : the
leather is said to be improved by the addition of a small
quantity of the bark of the Hemlock Spruce.

The Spanish Oak is adapted to the climate of the

centre of France, if we may judge from its multiplication in the nurseries and in the gardens of amateurs. The stocks that have sprung from the acorns which I sent home during my residence in America bear as yet only three-lobed leaves, but they will become falcated at a maturer age.

From the inferiority of its wood, this species would not, in my opinion, deserve a place in our forests, though its bark should prove equal to that of the European Oak. But in the Southern States, when some species of trees are to be multiplied in preference to others, the Spanish Oak alone should be spared among the Red Oaks, as, besides its superiority in other respects, it has the advantage of flourishing on lands of a middling quality, such as compose a large part of that Section of the United States.

PLATE XXIII.

A branch with leaves and fruit of the natural size.

Pl. 23.

Spanish Oak.

Quercus falcata.

BLACK OAK.

QUERCUS TINCTORIA. *Q. foliis profunde sinuosis, subtus pulverulentis; cupulâ turbinatâ, squamosâ; glande brevi ovatâ.*

EXCEPT the District of Maine, the northern part of New Hampshire, Vermont and Tennessee, this species is found throughout the United States on both sides of the Alleghanies, and it is every where called Black Oak. It is more abundant in the Middle States, and in the upper part of the Carolinas and Georgia, than on the southern coast.

The Black Oak flourishes in a poorer soil than the White Oak. In Maryland and certain districts of Virginia, where the soil is lean, gravelly and uneven, it is constantly united in the forests with the Scarlet, Spanish and Post Oaks, and the Mockernut Hickory, with which the Yellow Pine is also frequently mingled.

This Oak is one of the loftiest trees of North America, being 80 or 90 feet high and 4 or 5 feet in diameter. The leaves are large, deeply laciniated, and divided into four or five lobes : they resemble those of the Scarlet Oak, but have less deep and open sinuses, are less shining, of a duller green, and in the spring and during a part of the summer have their surface roughened with small glands which are sensible to the eye and to the touch. The same appearance is observed on the young shoots. I have remarked that the leaves of the young stocks change in the autumn to a dull red, and those of the old trees to yellow, beginning with the petiole.

The trunk is covered with a deeply furrowed bark of middling thickness, and always of a black or very deep brown colour, whence probably is derived the name of the tree. North-east of Pennsylvania the complexion of the bark is the only character by which it can be distinguished from the Red, Scarlet and Grey Oaks, when the leaves are fallen. Farther south this character is not sufficient to distinguish it from the Spanish Oak, whose bark is of the same colour, and recourse must be had to the buds, which, on the Black Oak, are longer, more acuminate, and more scaly. All doubt may be removed by chewing a bit of the cellular integument of each : that of the Black Oak is very bitter and gives a yellow tinge to the saliva, which is not the case with the other.

The wood is reddish and coarse-grained, with empty pores : it is, however, more esteemed for strength and durability than that of any other species of biennial fructification. At Philadelphia it is employed, for want of white oak, in building; and the farmers of the Northern States, by a miscalculating economy, substitute it in the place of the White Oak for fences.

As this species is abundant in the Northern and Middle States, it furnishes a large proportion of the

Red Oak staves exported to the Colonies or employed at home to contain flower, salted provisions and melasses.

The bark is extensively used in tanning, as it is easily procured and is rich in tannin. The only inconvenience which attends it is imparting a yellow colour to the leather, whieh must be discharged by a particular process, to prevent its staining the stockings : it is a great error to assert that this colour augments its value

From the cellular integument of the Black Oak is obtained the *quercitron*, of which great use is made in dying wool, silk and paper-hangings. According to several authors who have written on this subject, and among others Dr. Bancroft, to whom we are indebted for this discovery, one part of quercitron yields as much colouring matter as eight or ten parts of woad. The decoction is of a brownish yellow, which is rendered deeper by alkali, and lighter by acids. A solution of alum causes a small portion of the colouring matter to fall in a deep yellow precipitate; solutions of tin afford a more abundant precipitate of a bright hue.

To dye wool, it is sufficient to boil the quercitron with an equal weight of alum : in dipping the stuff, the deepest shade is given first, and afterwards the straw-colour: to animate the tint the stuff may be passed, in coming out of the dye, through water whitened with a little washed chalk. A brighter colour is obtained by means of a solution of tin. Quercitron may be substituted for woad, in giving all the shades of yellow to silk : the proportion is one part by weight to twelve parts of silk. In the advertisements of Philadelphia for February 1808, this substance is rated at 40 dollars a ton, and from that city chiefly it is exported to Europe.

Though the wood of the Black Oak is of a better quality than that of the Scarlet, Spanish, Red, Pin, Grey, Willow and Water Oaks, which are all comprehended under the name of *Red Oak*, it is much inferior to that of the European Oak. But its stature, the rapidity of its growth in the coldest climates and the most indifferent soils, and, above all, the value of its bark in dying, recommend it powerfully to the notice of European foresters.

PLATE XXIV.

A leaf of the natural size.

Note. *The small branch with the acorns belongs to the Scarlet Oak.*

Black·Oak.

Quercus tinctoria.

SCARLET OAK.

QUERCUS COCCINEA. *Q. foliis longe petiolatis, oblongis, profundè sinuatis, glabris; lobis dentatis, acutis; cupulá insigniter squamosá; glande brevi ovatá.*

THE Scarlet Oak is first seen in the vicinity of Boston, but it is less multiplied than in New Jersey, Pennsylvania, Virginia, and the upper part of the Carolinas and Georgia, where it forms a part of the forests that are still standing: it is much less common in the lower parts of these States, which, as I have already observed, produce nothing but Pines. I have not seen it in the district of Maine, the States of New Hampshire and Vermont, nor beyond Utica in Gennessee. In the Northern States it is confounded with the Red Oak, and in those of the South, with the Spanish Oak. The name of Scarlet Oak was given it by my father, and, though not in use among the inhabitants, it will probably be adopted, as the tree is evidently a distinct species.

This is a vegetable of more than 80 feet in height and of 3 or 4 feet in diameter. The leaves, which are supported by long petioles, are of a beautiful green, shining on both sides, and laciniated in a remarkable manner, having usually four deep sinuses very broad at the bottom. They begin to change with the first cold, and, after several successive frosts, turn to a bright red, in-

stead of a dull hue like those of the Red Oak. At this
season the singular colour of the foliage forms a striking
contrast with that of the surrounding trees, and is
itself a sufficient inducement to cultivate the tree for
ornament.

The acorns are large, somewhat elongated, similarly
rounded at both ends, and half covered with scaly
cups. As this fruit varies in size with the quality of the
soil, it is difficult to distinguish it from that of the Black
Oak; the only constant difference is in the kernel,
which is yellowish in the Black Oak, and white in the
species we are considering.

The wood of the Scarlet Oak is reddish and coarse-
grained, with open pores. As it decays much more rapidly than the White Oak, it is employed by the builder
and wheel-wright only from necessity or economy. It is
poor fuel, and is used principally for staves : in the
Middle States, a large part of the *Red Oak staves* are
furnished by this species.

The bark, though very thick and generally employed
in tanning, is in no respect preferable to that of the
Grey and Red Oaks.

That this tree will flourish in France, is shown by
an example at Rambouillet, where it makes part of a
beautiful plantation 45 feet in height, formed, in 1786,
of species sent home by my father soon after his arrival
in the United States. It is to be regretted that so fine a
tree, which is so well adapted to our soil, should afford

Pl. 25.

Scarlet Oak.

Quercus coccinea.

such indifferent wood that we cannot recommend its introduction into the forests of Europe, nor its preservation in those of the United States.

PLATE XXV.

A leaf of the natural size.

Note. *The acorns in this plate belong to the Black Oak.*

——

GREY OAK.

QUERCUS BOREALIS. *Q. foliis sinuatis, glabris, sinubus subacutis; cupulâ subscutellatâ; glande turgide ovatâ.*

THE Grey Oak appears, by my father's notes, to be found farther north than any other species in America; in returning from Hudson's Bay he saw it on the St. Lawrence between Quebec and Malabaie, in latitude 47° 50′. Under that parallel, and near Halifax in Nova Scotia, where I first observed it, it is not more than 40 feet high; and, though the bloom is annual, the winter is so rigorous and so long that the fruit is said to be matured only once in three or four years. Three degrees farther south in Maine and New Hampshire, and on the shores of Lake Champlain in Vermont, it is more multiplied, and is 50 or 60 feet in height and 18 inches in diameter. It is called by the inhabitants Grey Oak, but it has been confounded by botanists with the Red Oak, to which it bears a close analogy in its foliage, as it does to the Scarlet Oak in its fruit : on this resemblance I have founded the latin specific name *ambigua.*

The leaves are large, smooth, and deeply sinuated at right angles to the main rib. The acorns are of the middle size, rounded at the end, and contained in scaly cups.

The wood is similar to that of the other species in-

Gray Oak.

Quercus ambigua.

cluded under the common name of Red Oak. Its coarse
and open texture renders it unfit for any use except to
contain dry wares ; but in districts where Oak wood is
rare, recourse is had, for other purposes, to several
species of inferior quality, which are still preferred to
the Birch, the Beech, and the Pine. Thus the Grey Oak
is employed for the knees of vessels and for cartwrights'
work ; it is even preferred to the Red Oak, as being
stronger and more durable.

This tree is without interest, as the regions in which
it grows possess other species in every respect preferable, such as the White Oak, the Swamp White Oak,
and the Rock Chesnut Oak.

PLATE XXVI.

A branch with leaves and fruit of the natural size.

PIN OAK.

QUERCUS PALUSTRIS. *Q. foliis profunde sinuatis, glabris, sinubus latis; fructu parvo; cupulâ scutellatâ, lævi; glande subglobosâ.*

THIS species, like the preceding, grows in Massachusetts, but is less common than in the vicinity of New York, in New Jersey, Pennsylvania and Maryland. I saw it abundant beyond the mountains near Pittsburgh in Ohio, and in East Tennesse, and my father found it multiplied in the country of the Illinois : I feel assured that it does not exist in Maine, Vermont and the Southern States. It is called Pin Oak in the lower part of New York and in New Jersey, and Swamp Spanish Oak in Pennsylvania, Delaware and Maryland. The last of these denominations is sufficiently appropriate ; but I have preferred the second, because it is less liable to mistake, and is indicative of a characteristic arrangement of the branches.

The Pin Oak is a tall tree, which grows constantly in moist places, and of preference about the swamps enclosed in the forests. In these situations it is frequently more than 80 feet high and 3 or 4 feet in diameter. Its secondary branches are more slender and numerous than is common on so large a tree, and are intermingled so as to give it at a distance the appearance of being

stuffed. This singular disposition renders it distinguishable at first sight in the winter, and is perhaps the cause
of its being called Pin Oak.

The leaves are smooth, of a pleasing green, supported by long petioles, deeply laciniated and very
similar to those of the Scarlet Oak, from which they
differ principally in their proportions. The acorns are
small, round, and contained in flat shallow cups,
of which the scales are closely applied one upon
another.

The bark upon the oldest trunk is scarcely cracked,
and consists almost wholly of a very thick cellular integument. The wood is coarse-grained, with the pores
open and larger than those of the Scarlet and Red
Oaks : though stronger and more tenacious than those
species, it is little esteemed for durability. It is used for
the axle-trees of mill-wheels when White Oak of sufficient dimensions cannot be procured; it is also sometimes, though rarely, made into staves, as the species
is little multiplied compared with the Scarlet, Red and
Black Oaks.

The Pin Oak, in its youth, assumes an agreeable
pyramidal shape, and its light elegant foliage contributes
greatly to its beauty. It deserves a conspicuous place
in parks and gardens. It should never be deprived of its
interior branches. The most beautiful stock of this species with which I am acquainted in Europe, is in a garden near Antwerp; it was about 20 feet high in 1804,

and its brilliant and vigorous vegetation proved how
well it was suited in the soil and climate.

PLATE XXVII.

A branch with leaves and fruit of the natural size.

Pl. 27.

ute del

Gabriel Sc

Pin Oak.

Quercus palustris.

RED OAK.

QUERCUS RUBRA. *Q. foliis longe petiolatis, glabris, obtuse sinuatis; cupulâ scutellatâ, sublœvi; glande subovatâ.*

NEXT to the Grey Oak this species is found in the highest latitude of all the American Oaks, and is one of the most common species in the Northern States and in Canada. Farther south, particularly in the lower part of New York, in New Jersey, the upper Districts of Pennsylvania, and along the whole range of the Alleghanies, it is nearly as abundant as the Scarlet and Black Oaks; but it is much less common in Maryland, lower Virginia, and the maritime parts of the Carolinas and Georgia. This remark confirms an observation which I have often made, that its perfect developement requires a cool climate and a fertile soil. It is universally known by the name of Red Oak, except near Lancaster in Pennsylvania, where it is sometimes confounded with the Spanish Oak.

The Red Oak is a tall, wide-spreading tree, frequently more than 80 feet high, and 3 or 4 feet in diameter. Its leaves are smooth and shining on both sides, large, deeply laciniated, and rounded at the base : they are larger and have deeper and narrower sections on the young stock than on the middle or the summit of the full-grown tree : these last resemble the leaves of the Spanish Oak, which, however, are always downy beneath, while those of the Red Oak are perfectly smooth. In the autumn they change to a dull red, and turn yellow before they fall.

The acorns are very large and abundant, rounded at the summit, compressed at the base, and contained in flat cups covered with narrow compact scales. They are voraciously devoured by wild animals, and by the cows, horses and swine which are allowed to range in the woods after the herbage has perished.

The wood is reddish and coarse - grained, and the pores are often large enough for the passage of a hair : it is strong but not durable, and is the last among the Oaks to be employed in building. Its principal use is for staves, which, at home, are used to contain salted provisions, flour, and other dry wares that are exported to the islands, and, in the Colonies, to receive melasses and sugar.

The bark consists of a very thin epidermis and a very thick cellular integument. It is extensively used in tanning, but is less esteemed than that of the Spanish, Black and Rock Chesnut Oaks.

The Red Oak was one of the earliest American trees introduced into Europe. Large stocks are found on the estate of Duhamel, which yield seed abundantly, and even multiply naturally; but the quality of its wood is so inferior, that I cannot recommend its propagation in our forests.

PLATE XXVIII.

A branch with leaves and fruit of the natural size.

P.J. Redouté del.

Red Oak.

Quercus rubra.

ADDITIONS TO THE OAKS.

In the botanical work of F. Pursh, *Flora Americæ Septentrionalis,* published in England in 1814, the following species of Oak are added to those which I have described.

QUERCUS MARITIMA. *Q. foliis perennantibus, coriaceis, integerrimis, glabris, basi attenuatis, apice mucronatis; cupulá scutellatá; glande subrotundá.*

A shrub from 3 to 8 feet high, found on the sea-coast in Virginia and Carolina: I consider it as a variety of the Willow Oak, *Quercus phellos.*

QUERCUS MYRTIFOLIA. *Q. foliis perennantibus, coriaceis, oblongis, integerrimis, glabris, utrinque acutis, supra nitidis, margine revolutis.*

This species, of which Mr. Pursh appears to have seen neither the blossoms nor the acorns, escaped my researches; perhaps it is the variety of the Water Oak which I found among the Live Oaks and which preserves its leaves for three or four years.

QUERCUS HEMISPHÆRICA. *Q. foliis perennantibus, oblongo-lanceolatis, trilobis sinuatisque, lobis mucronatis, utrinque glabris.* Willd.

Mr. Pursh has inserted this species from Willdenow, and he believes it to be a variety of the Water Oak, *Quercus aquatica.*

QUERCUS NANA. *Q. foliis cuneiformis, glabris, apice tri-lobis, basi subsinuatis, lobis, divaricatis, mucronatis, inter-medio majore; cupulâ scutellatâ.*

According to Mr. Pursh, this species is a low-growing shrub, distinct from the Water Oak, *Quercus aquatica.*

QUERCUS DISCOLOR. *Q. foliis oblongis, pinnatifido-si-nuatis, subtus pubescentibus, lobis oblongis, dentatis, seta-ceo-mucronatis; cupulâ turbinatâ.*

This species of Mr. Pursh I consider as a variety of the *Quercus tinctoria.*

OAKS found in New Spain by Messrs. Humboldt and Bonpland, and described in their Nova Genera et Spe-cies Plantarum. PARIS, 1816.

QUERCUS CONFERTIFOLIA. *Q. ramulis abbreviatis; foliis brevissime petiolatis, confertis, lanceolatis, acuminatis, mucronato-aristatis, integerrimis, coriaceis; margine sub-reflexis, subtus pubescentibus; fructibus subgeminis, sessi-libus.*

This tree is 10 or 12 feet in height : it is evergreen, grows in the temperate and mountainous regions of New Spain, between Guanaxuato and Santa Rosa, and fructifies in September.

QUERCUS CRASSIPES. *Q. ramulis tuberculosis; foliis bre-viter petiolatis, lanceolato-oblongis, mucronatis, basi ro-tundatis, integerrimis, coriaceis, subtus cinereo-tomentosis; fructibus pedunculatis, subgeminis; pedunculis incrassatis; cupulis subturbinatis.*

This tree is about 20 feet high ; it is found on the low mountains of New Spain, near Santa Rosa, and fructifies in September and October.

QUERCUS MEXICANA. *Q. ramulis foliisque, subtus stellatim pubescentibus, supra nitidis, lineari-oblongis, acutis, submucronatis, subcordatis, undulato-subsinuatis, subcoriaceis; fructibus solitariis, breviter pedunculatis; cupulis cyathiformibus.*

This species rises from 15 to 20 feet ; it is very abundant between Acapulco and the city of Mexico, near Moxonera, Quaxiniquilapa and Chilpancingo, and is also found near Moran, Regla, Guanaxuato and Santa Rosa : it fructifies in September.

QUERCUS LANCEOLATA. *Q. ramulis tuberculatis; foliis oblongo-lanceolatis, utrinque acutis, undulato-repandis, coriaceis, supra nitidis, subtus stellatim pubescentibus; fructibus subternis, brevissime pedunculatis; cupulis cyathiformibus.*

This tree equals, and sometimes exceeds, 20 feet in height : it abounds in the temperate regions of Mexico between Moran and Santa Rosa, where it forms immense forests : it fructifies in September.

QUERCUS TRIDENS. *Q. ramis lævibus; foliis oblongis, basi rotundatis, apice cuspidato-tridentatis, membranaceis, supra pubescentibus, subtus tenuiter cinereo-tomentosis; fructibus ternis aut quinis, breviter pedunculatis.*

This tree rises from 10 to 20 feet ; it grows in the mountains near Moran in Mexico, and fructifies in May.

QUERCUS LAURINA. *Q. ramulis glabris; foliis oblongis, acuminatis, basi subrotundatis; apicem versus subdentatis, coriaceis, glabris, nitidis; fructibus solitariis aut ternis, sessilibus; cupulis cyathiformibus.*

This is a large tree, which resembles the Laurel, and attains the height of 40 feet : it is found in the temperate parts of New Spain, in the environs of Pachuca, Totonilco and Grande : it flowers in May.

QUERCUS REPANDA. *Q. fructicosa procumbens; ramulis foliisque subtus albido-tomentosis, subsessilibus, oblongis, obtusiusculis, basi inæqualibus, sinuato-repandis, coriaceis; fructibus subsolitariis, sessilibus.*

This is a shrub about 2 feet in height : it grows in moist shady situations, between Real del Monte and Moran, and flowers in May.

QUERCUS DEPRESSA. *Q. fructicosa, procumbens; ramulis pubescentibus; foliis sempervirentibus, oblongis, acutis, basi rotundatis, argute et remote dentatis, rigidis, glabris, nitidis; fructibus geminis aut ternis, breviter pedunculatis.*

This species is an evergreen shrub, numerously ramified, and only 1 or 2 feet in height : it abounds in the same situations with the preceding, and flowers in May and June.

QUERCUS CHRYSOPHYLLA. *Q. ramulis sulcatis, pubescentibus; foliis oblongis, basi rotundatis, apicem versus cuspidato-dentatis, membranaceis, supra nitidis, subtus tenuissime aureo-tomentosis; fructibus ternis aut quinis, pedunculatis.*

This tree, which has a thin foliage, rises to the height of 30 or 40 feet, and is from 18 to 24 inches in diameter: it grows in the temperate and stony parts of New Spain between Moran, Pachuca and Regla, and flowers in May.

QUERCUS XALAPENSIS. *Q. ramis tuberculatis; foliis longe petiolatis, ovato-oblongis, acuminatis, remote cuspidato-dentatis, subcoriaceis, glabris; fructibus solitariis aut geminis, breviter pedunculatis; cupulis cyathiformibus.*

This is a very lofty tree about 2 feet in diameter: it is very common in the forests near Xalapa, on the eastern side of the mountains; it fructifies in January.

QUERCUS ACUTIFOLIA. *Q. foliis ovato-lanceolatis, acuminatis, inæqualiter subcordatis, subtus pulverulento-tomentosis, ferrugineis, sinuato-dentatis; dentibus elongatis; cuspidatis; fructibus geminis aut quaternis, brevissime pedunculatis.*

A very lofty tree, about 2 feet in diameter, which grows on the west side of the mountains between Venta di Acaguisolta and la Majonera: it fructifies in May.

QUERCUS STIPULARIS. *Q. ramulis ferrugineo-tomentosis; foliis obovato-oblongis, subcordatis, argute et grosse dentatis; crasse coriaceis, supra nitidis, subtus flavido-tomentosis; stipulis persistentibus; fructibus solitariis aut geminis, sessilibus.*

This tree rises to the height of about 50 feet, and has a thick foliage: it is found on the mountains of Mexico near Actopan, and fructifies in May.

QUERCUS SYDEROXYLA. *Q. ramulis pubescentibus; foliis*

obovato-oblongis, basi rotundatis, apicem versus argute
serratis, cordatis, remote et oblise dentatis, membranaceis,
subtus tomentosis; fructibus longe pedunculatis, subspicatis;
cupulis hemisphæricis.

A very lofty tree from 1 to 2 feet in diameter; it grows
in the temperate regions of New Spain near Villalpando
and Santa Rosa, and fructifies in September.

QUERCUS PULCHELLA. *Q. ramis tuberculatis; foliis obovato-oblongis, subcordatis, argute dentatis, coriaceis, supra
nitidis, subtus tenuissime incano-tomentosis; fructibus geminis, breviter pedunculatis; cupulis depresso-sphæricis.*

This tree is from 15 to 20 feet in height and grows in
the mountainous regions of New Spain between Guanaxuato and Santa Rosa; it fructifies in September.

QUERCUS RETICULATA. *Q. ramulis subpubescentibus; foliis subsessilibus, obovatis, cordatis, remote dentatis, coriaceis, rugosis, subtus tenuissime tomentosis; fructibus geminis, longe pedunculatis; cupulis cyathiformibus.*

A tall tree which grows in the mountainous regions of
New Spain between Santa Rosa and Guanaxuato, and
fructifies in September.

QUERCUS CRASSIFOLIA. *Q. ramulis sulcatis, foliisque subtus flavescenti-tomentosis, breviter petiolatis, obovatis, cordatis, remote dentatis, crasse coriaceis; fructibus subternis,
pedunculatis; cupulis subsphæricis.*

This tree is from 30 to 40 feet high, and has a very thick
foliage; it is found in the stony and mountainous regions
of New Spain near Chilpancingo, and fructifies in April.

QUERCUS SPICATA. *Q. ramulis tomentosis; foliis ellipti-*
cis, sinuato-dentatis, coriaceis, supra nitidis, subtus tenuis-
sime canescenti-tomentosis; fructibus subgeminis, brevissime
pedunculatis; cupulis cyathiformibus.

This species is from 30 to 40 feet in height, and is
found in shady situations near el Oyamel, el Jacal, and
Cerro de las Nabajas: it fructifies in May.

QUERCUS PANDURATA. *Q. ramulis lævibus, hirtis; foliis*
obovato-oblongis, subpanduratis, subcordatis, sinuato-den-
tatis, coriaceis, subtus pubescentibus; fructibus subquinis,
pedunculatis; cupulis cyathiformibus.

This species is about 15 feet high: it is found on the
sides of the mountains in the kingdom of Mechoacán,
between Ario and Patzcuaro: it fructifies in September.

QUERCUS AMBIGUA. *Q. ramulis glabris, obovato-oblon-*
gis, obtusis, basi rotundatis, subrepandis, membranaceis,
subtus tenuissime pubescentibus; fructibus quinis aut septe-
nis, peduncúlatis, pedunculis geminis, elongatis.

This tree is about 20 feet high, and is found in the
temperate regions of Mexico near Moran, Cerro Ven-
toso and Omilton: it flowers in May.

QUERCUS GLAUCESCENS. *Q. ramulis angulatis; foliis bre-*
vissime petiolatis, obovato-oblongis, obtusiusculis, basi cu-
neatis, dentato-sinuatis, membranaceis, glabris, glaucescen-
tibus; fructibus quinis aut septenis, pedunculatis.

A tall tree, very common in the warm parts of New
Spain, between la Venta de la Majorena and Acagui-
sotla: it blooms in April.

QUERCUS OBTUSATA. *Q. ramulis tuberculatis, tenuiter pubescentibus; foliis oblongis, obtusis, basi inæqualibus, repandis, coriaceis, subtus pulverulento-pubescentibus; fructibus subquinis, pedunculatis; cupulis campanulato-globosis.*

This species is very tall, with a remarkably straight trunk: it is found in the elevated and dry parts of New Spain near Ario, and flowers in September.

WALNUTS.

THE
NORTH AMERICAN
SYLVA,

OR

A DESCRIPTION OF THE FOREST TREES,

OF THE

UNITED STATES, CANADA AND NOVA SCOTIA.

Considered particularly with respect to their use in the Arts
and their introduction into Commerce;

TO WHICH IS ADDED

A DESCRIPTION OF THE MOST USEFUL OF THE EUROPEAN FOREST TREES.

ILLUSTRATED BY 150 COLOURED ENGRAVINGS.

By F. ANDREW MICHAUX,

Member of the American Philosophical Society of Philadelphia; of the Royal
Agricultural Society, Correspondent of the Institute of France, etc.

SECOND HALF VOLUME.

·

PHILADELPHIA,

Sold by THOMAS DOBSON. — SOLOMON CONRAD.

PARIS, PRINTED BY C. D'HAUTEL.

1817.

N. For the translation of the present half volume, I am indebted to my friend AUGUSTUS L. HILLHOUSE, *of Connecticut.* F. A. M.

WALNUTS.

In the variety of trees which compose the vast forests of North America east of the Mississippi, the Walnut ranks after the oak, among the genera whose species are most multiplied. In this particular, the soil of the United States is more favoured than that of Europe, to no part of which is any species of this tree indigenous. I have distinguished in the United States ten species of Walnut, and others will probably be discovered in Louisiana : travellers who visit these regions to explore their natural history, should direct their attention to this class of vegetables, so interesting from the useful applications of their wood in the arts. There is room to hope, also, that species may be discovered, susceptible, like the Pacanenut Hickory, of speedy melioration, by the aid of grafting and of attentive cultivation. Some weight is given this consideration, by an observation which I have heard often repeated by my father, that the fruit of the Common European Walnut, in its natural state, is harder than that of the American species just mentioned, and inferior to it in size and quality. To the members of agricultural societies in the United States it belongs, to extend their observations and experiments on this subject, after the example of our ancestors, to whom we are indebted for a rich variety of fruits, equally salutary and beautiful. .

The Walnuts of North America appear to present characters so distinct as to require their division into two sections. These characters consist principally in the form of the barren aments or catkins, and in the greater or less rapidity of vegetation in the trees. The first section is composed of Walnuts with single aments, (Pl. 29 and 30) and includes two species : the Black Walnut and the Butternut; to which is added the European Walnut. The second section consists of such as have compound aments, (Pl. 36) and comprises eight species: the Pacanenut Hickory, Bitternut Hickory, Water Bitternut Hickory, Mockernut Hickory, Shellbark Hickory, Thick Shellbark Hickory, Pignut Hickory, and Nutmeg Hickory. The three first species of the second section bear some relation to those of the first, in their buds, which are not covered with scales. For this reason, I have placed them immediately next, beginning with the Pacanenut Hickory, which by its nu-

merous leaflets, most nearly resembles the Black
Walnut and the Butternut, whose buds are also uncovered.

Throughout the United States, the common name of
Hickory is given to the species of the second section.
This common appellation is due to certain properties
of their wood, which, howerer modified, are possessed
by them all, in a greater degree than by any other
tree of Europe or America. These species exhibit also
a striking analogy in their form, and in their leaves,
though they differ in the number and size of their leaflets. To these sources of confusion, must be added
another in the fruit, which is often so various in its appearance, that it is easy to mistake the species to which
it belongs. It is not then, on the most remarkable
differences alone, that our distinctions must be founded ; recourse must also be had to an examination of
the shoots of the preceding year, of the buds, and of
the aments. It was only by constant observation in the
forests of the country, pursued through the course of
a summer, that I became able readily to distinguish
between mere varieties and species. M. Delille of the
Institute of Egypt, who was at that time in the United
States, took an active part in my researches, and re-

sorted with me daily to the woods. Our investigations,
I flatter myself, have had the result, which may always
be hoped for, from unwearied perseverance.

From the considerations alleged, and principally
from the striking resemblance of their wood, I have
thought proper in describing the species of Hickory,
to speak but summarily of their respective properties,
and to treat of this part of the subject collectively and
comparatively, more at large, in a separate article which
will complete their history.

METHODICAL DISPOSITION

OF THE WALNUTS

OF NORTH AMERICA.

Monœcia Polyandria, LINN. *Terebenthaceæ* , JUSS.

I.ˢᵗ SECTION.

Simple aments. (*Pl.* 29 *and* 3o.)

VEGETATION RAPID.

1. Common European Walnut. *Juglans regia.*
2. Black Walnut. . . . . . . *Juglans nigra.*
3. Butternut. . . . . · . . . *Juglans cathartica.*

2.ⁿᵈ SECTION.

Compound aments , each peduncle bearing three.
(*Pl.* 36 , *fig.* 3.)

VEGETATION SLOW.

4. Pacanenut Hickory . . . . *Juglans olivæformis.*
5. Bitternut Hickory. . . . . *Juglans amara.*
6. Water Bitternut Hickory. . *Juglans aquatica.*
7. Mockernut Hickory. . · . *Juglans tomentosa.*

8. Shellbark Hickory. . . . . *Juglans squamosa.*
9. Thick shellbark Hickory. . . *Juglans laciniosa.*
10. Pignut Hickory. . . . . . *Juglans porcina.*
11. Nutmeg Hickory. . . . . . *Juglans myristicæformis.*

Pl. 29

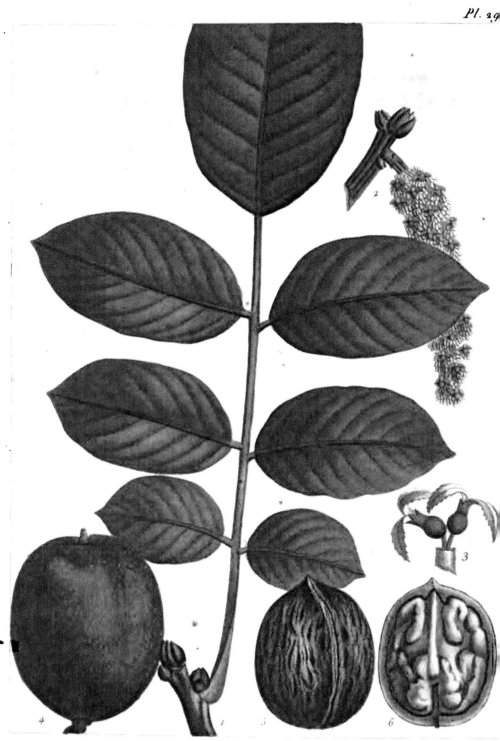

Common European Walnut.
Juglans regia.

COMMON EUROPEAN WALNUT.

JUGLANS REGIA. *J. foliolis subseptenis, ovalibus, glabris, sub-serratis, subæqualibus: fructibus subovalibus.*

The Walnut which for several centuries has been cultivated in Europe is a native of Asia. According to an ancient but uncertain tradition, its fruit was brought from Persia with the Peach and the Apricot. My father, who in the years 1782, 83, and 84, visited this part of the East to examine its natural productions, first ascertained with exactness, the origin of this tree : he found it in the natural State, in the Province of Ghilan, which lies on the Caspian Sea, between the 35° and the 40° of latitude.

The period of its introduction into Europe, a point on which ancient authors leave us in obscurity, is proved to be remote, by several rites in use among the Romans : such, for instance, as the distribution of nuts in the *Cerealia*. In the village festival of the *Rosière*, instituted by St. Médard, at Salency, Department of the Oise, 1200 years ago, it is directed, that an offering be presented to the young maid who is crowned, composed of nuts and other fruits of the Country : which proves the tree to have been already naturalised in that part of France.

The Walnut is common throughout the center of Europe, but it flourishes most in the western and southern Deparments of France, in Spain and in Italy, which approach nearest to the latitude in which it grows in the natural state. In France, it is only in the West and South, that the vegetation of the Walnut is perfectly secure from frost, that its wood is of a superior quality, and that its fruit is regularly yielded in sufficient abundance to become an article of commerce.

The European Walnut is one of the tallest and most beautiful among fruit trees, and one of the most remarkable for the amplitude of its summit, and the thickness of its shade. On the trunk of old trees, which frequently are several feet in diameter, the bark is thick and deeply furrowed; on the upper branches, it is grey and smooth, a good deal resembling that of the Butternut. The leaves are borne by long petioles, and are composed of 2, 3, and sometimes 4 pair of leaflets, surmounted by an odd one. The leaflets are oval and smooth; when bruised, they exhale a strong aromatic odour. In the extreme heat of summer, the emanations from the Walnut are so powerful as to produce unpleasant effects upon some persons, if they slumber in its shade.

The flowers of the Common European Walnut, like those of the Black Walnut and Butternut, appear before the unfolding of the leaves; the barren ones in single, pendulous, imbricated aments; the fertile ones on separate branches, at the end of the young shoots, and commonly in pairs. The fruit is green and oval, and in the natural state contains a small hard nut. In the most esteemed cultivated species, the fruit is oval and strongly odoriferous, about an inch and two thirds long, and from an inch and a quarter to an inch and a half in diameter. The nut occupies two thirds of its volume.

Towards autumn, the husk softens, and decaying from about the nut, allows it to fall. The shell is slightly channeled, and so thin as to be easily crushed by the fingers. The kernel is of a very agreeable taste : it is large, covered with a fine pellicle, and separated by a thin partition which may readily be detached both from the shell and from the kernel. The nuts are better tasted and easier of digestion, soon after their maturity, than later in the season, when the oily principle becomes perfectly formed; they are then oppressive if immoderately eaten.

A dessert of an excellent relish is made by extracting the kernels a fortnight before they are ripe, and seasoning them with the juice of green grapes and salt. They should be thrown into water as soon as they are taken from the shell, and allowed to remain till the moment when they are seasoned to be set upon the table. They are sold in Paris by the name of Cerneaux, and a greater quantity of walnuts is consumed in this way by people in easy circumstances, than after they are perfectly ripe : the use of them is then almost exclusively confined to the lower classes.

I. 19

The Common Walnut is more multiplied in the Departments of France which lie between the 45° and the 48° of latitude, than in any other part of Europe. In these Departments, it is planted in the midst of cultivated fields, like the apple tree for cider, in those of the north and of the center : the fruit, the oil, and the wood, may be considered as forming one of their principal branches of commerce.

In extracting the oil of Walnuts, certain delicate attentions are necessary to insure its fineness. When the fruit is gathered, and the nuts are separated from the husks, they should be kept dry, and occasionally moved till they are used. The properest time for the operation is at the close of winter, as in this interval, the change by which the mucilage of the fruit is converted into oil has become completely effected, and by longer delay the kernel grows rancid, and the oil is of a vitiated quality. The nut is cracked by striking it on the end with a small mallet, and pains are taken not to bruise the kernel. The slight ligneous partition is detached, and such kernels as are partially spoiled, are selected and thrown aside. The sound kernels, thus cleared from every particle of the shell, should be sent immediately to the mill, as they soon become rancid by exposure to the air. They are crushed by a vertical stone, which turns in a circular trough, and is moved by a horse or by a current of water. The paste is next enclosed in bags of strong linen and submitted to the press. The oil which flows under this first pressure without the application of heat, is of the best quality. It is very clear, and is proper for food; but it sensibly retains the taste of the nut, which in general is not agreeable to persons unaccustomed to it, so that the consumption is limited to the Departments where it is made. To be kept sweet for the table, it should be drawn off several times during the first months, carefully corked, and kept in the cellar, as it is more easily affected than any other oil by the action of air and heat.

After the first expression, the paste is emptied from the sacks, moistened with warm water, and moderately heated in coppers. It is then replaced in the sacks and returned to the press. The oil of the second discharge, is highly coloured, and very speedily becomes rancid; it is therefore employed only in the preparation of colours. The cakes which remain after the expression is finished, are proper for fattening fowls.

Although nut oil, as an article of diet, is in general use in the Departments where the tree abounds, it serves a still more important purpose in the preparation of fine colours. It is preferred on account of the complete and rapid manner in which it dries, and of the facility of obtaining it perfectly limpid; which is done by diffusing it upon water in large shallow vases.

In copper-plate printing, walnut oil is considered, in

Paris, indispensably necessary for a fine impression, in black or in colours. But there are peculiar modes of preparing it for the several colours with which it is to be mixed. Thus for white, blue, light green, and the intermediate shades, it is reduced by boiling to two thirds of its bulk, but for dark green and black, to one fifth, which leaves it a thick, semifluid substance. To facilitate the process, one tenth part of linseed oil is added to it; it is then placed in an iron or copper vessel, over an active, clear fire. When it begins to boil rapidly, the vessel is uncovered, and the oil takes fire by contact with the flame, and burns till it is reduced to the proper consistency : sometimes it is not allowed to kindle, but when the ebullition commences, crusts of bread are thrown into it, which remain till the necessary evaporation is effected, and are then taken out, charged with mucilagenous particles. The principal advantage of this oil, in the preparation of white lead for painting the interior of houses, as well as of the colours employed in copper-plate printing, is the longer and more perfect preservation of the tints. The back of prints done with it do not turn yellow like others.

A fine stomachic liquor is made with the fruit of the Walnut gathered a month before its maturity. Twelve green nuts in the husk are bruised and thrown into a pint of good brandy; after they have steeped three weeks, the brandy is filtered through brown paper, and a quarter of a pound of loaf sugar is added. This cordial improves by age.

Diers obtain by boiling the husks, when they begin to decay, and the bark of the roots, a substantial dark brown, with which they die woolens. Cabinet-makers also make use of it, in staining other species of wood in imitation of Walnut.   •

Among the American Walnuts which are found east of the Mississippi, the Black Walnut bears the greatest resemblance to the European Walnut, in its general appearance, in its flowers and fruit, and in the qualities of its wood : in foliage they are strikingly different. The wood of the European Walnut is inferior in strength and weight, and I believe, far more liable to injury from worms.

Twenty or thirty years ago, before Mahogany was imported in such abundance into Europe, Walnut wood was employed almost exclusively, in Cabinet-making. In the country, it is still in general use, and the furniture made of it is far from being inelegant, especially, pieces obtained from such old trees as bear small and thick shelled nuts. It is preferred for the stocks of muskets; and in Paris and Brussels, no other wood is used for the pannels of carriages. The old trees furnisch excellent screws for large presses. Great quantities of wooden shoes are manufactured of Walnut, which are more highly esteemed than others.

The wood of the European Walnut is largely exported

from the south of France to the North, and to Holland and Germany : formerly, it was carried to England.

Like other fruit trees, whose perfection is among the « noblest conquests of industrious man », the Walnut has been greatly improved, by long and careful cultivation. There are 7 or 8 cultivated varieties, whose superiority is principally apparent in the augmented size of the fruit, and in the diminished thickness of the shell. Of these the most esteemed, after that which I have described, are the *St. Jean* and the *Jauge* Walnuts. The St. John Walnut, is a variety obtained within a few years. It yields fruit as large and as abundant as the common Walnut, and for that part of Europe which lies beyond the 45° of latitude, it possesses an advantage, in opening its vegetation three weeks later, and in being thus secure from the injuries of frost. The *Jauge* Walnut is chiefly remarkable for the size of its fruit, which is twice as large as the variety represented in the plate. It is unproductive, and the kernel does not fill the shell. The *Jauge* nut is made into cases by jewellers, and furnished with trinkets for the amusement of children.

The wood of the Black Walnut is already superior to that of the European Walnut, and it will acquire a still finer grain, when it is raised on lands that have been long under cultivation. It is solely for the excellency of its fruit, and the decided superiority of its oil in the preparation of colours, that the European

Walnut should be warmly recommended to the attention of Americans. It would thrive better than elsewhere in places where the Black Walnut naturally abounds.

In some parts of Pensylvania and Maryland , the Black Walnuts have been preserved in clearing the lands: great advantage would be found in grafting them with the European Walnut. The limbs should be cut 15 inches from the trunk, and from the stumps will spring vigorous shoots, which the second year may the grafted by inoculation. Fifty or sixty buds shonld be set upon each tree, as is practised near Lyons; where it is found, that by inserting the Walnut of St. John on the common Walnut, the fruit is rendered finer, and the crop more certain. Black Walnuts thus grafted begin to bear the 5.ᵗʰ year. On estates where no Black Walnuts exist, the deficiency may be supplied by planting the nuts, and grafting the young stocks when they come to the height of 8 or 10 feet.

It should be observed , that in the Walnut, more than any other tree , it is necessary on account of the loose texture of the wood and the large volume of the pith, to protect the amputated limbs from the weather. A covering of clay should be so nicely adapted to the exposed surface, as entirely to exclude the rain , otherwise decay will commence, and spread itself into the body of the tree.

In those parts of France , Belgium and Germany, where the Walnut is not cultivated for commerce , the trees have generally sprung from the seed, which is the cause of the inferiority of their fruit. For it is observed that, with a few accidental exceptions, the finest fruits and flowers degenerate in reproduction. This inconvenience would be experienced in the United States, and as there do not perhaps exist in that Country, south of the Hudson river, ten European Walnut trees, I should recommend the obtaining from Bordeaux of young grafted trees, which will soon furnish the means to such proprietors as wish to enrich their estates with this useful and magnificent tree.

PLATE XXIX.

Fig. 1, A leaf of half the natural size. Fig. 2, Barren flowers. Fig. 3, Fertile flowers. Fig. 4, A nut in its husk of the natural size. Fig. 5, A nut without its husk. Fig. 6, A nut deprived of half the shell to show the kernel.

Black Walnut.

BLACK WALNUT.

Juglans nigra. J. *foliolis quindenis, subcordatis, supernè angustatis, serratis: fructu globoso, punctato, scabriusculo; nuce corrugatâ.*

This tree is known in all parts of the United States where it grows, and to the french of Upper and Lower Louisiana, by no other name than Black Walnut. East of the Alleghany Mountains, the most Northern point at which it appears, is about Goshen in the Sate of New-Jersey, in the latitude of 40.° 50'. West of the Mountains, it exists abundantly two degrees farther north, in that portion of Genesee, which is comprised between the 77° and 79° of longitude. This observation, as I shall have occasion to remark, is applicable to several other vegetables, the northern limit of whose appearance varies with the climate, and this becomes milder in advancing towards the West. The Black Walnut is multiplied in the forests about Philadelphia, and with the exception of the lower parts of the Southern States, where the soil is too sandy, or too wet as in the Swamps, it is met with to the banks of the Mississippi, throughout an extent of 2000 miles. East of the Alleghany mountains in Virginia, and in the upper parts of the Carolinas and of Georgia, it is chiefly confined to vallies where the soil is deep and fertile, and which are watered by

1.

20

Creeks and Rivers: in the Western Country, in Genesee
and in the States of Ohio and Kentucky, where the soil
in general is very rich, it grows in the forests, with
the Coffee-tree, Honey Locust, Red Mulberry? Locust,
Shellbark Hickory, Black Sugar Maple, Hack Berry,
and Red Elm; all of them trees that prove the good-
ness of the soil in which they are found.

It is in these Countries that the Black Walnut dis-
plays its full proportions. On the banks of the Ohio
and on the Islands of this beautiful river, I have
often seen trees of 3 or 4 feet in diameter and 60 or
70 feet in height. It is not rare to find them of the
thickness of 6 or 7 feet. Its powerful vegetation clearly
points out this, as one of the largest trees of America. When it stands insulated, its branches, extending themselves horizontally to a great distance, spread
into a spacious head, which gives it a very majestic
appearance.

The leaves of the Black Walnut when bruised emit
a strong aromatic odour. They are about 18 inches in
length, pinnate, and composed in general of 6, 7, or
8 pair of leaflets surmounted by an odd one. The leaflets are opposite and fixed on short petioles; they are
acuminate, serrate, and somewhat downy. The barren
flowers are disposed in pendulous and cylindrical aments,
of which the peduncles are simple, unlike those of
the Hickories. (Pl. 3o. fig. 1.) The fruit is round, odoriferous, of rather an uneven surface, and always ap-

pears at the extremity of the branches : on young, and
vigorous trees, it is sometimes 7 or 8 inches in circumference. The husk is thick, and is not as in the Hickories
divided into sections ; but when ripe it softens and gradually decays. The nut is hard, somewhat compressed
at the sides, and sulcated. The kernel, which is divided by firm ligneous partitions , is of a sweet and
agreeable taste, thoug inferior to that of the European
Walnut. These nuts are sold in the markets of New-York,
Philadelphia, and Baltimore, and served upon the tables. The size of the fruit varies considerably, and de-
pends upon the vigour of the tree, and upon the nature
of the soil and of the climate. On the banks of the
Ohio, and in Kentucky, the fruit with the husk is 7 or
8 inhes in compass with the nut proportionally large :
in Genesee on the contrary, where the cold is intense,
and in fields exhausted by cultivation, where these trees
have been preserved since the first clearing of the land,
it is not of more than half this bigness. Some variations are observed in the form of the fruit, and in the
moulding of the shell ; but these I consider as merely,
accidental differences. Indeed there is no genus of trees
in America, in which the fruit of a given species exhibits such various forms, as in the Walnut ; and doubtless
this circumstance has mislead observers, who, being
acquainted only with the small number of trees existing
in European gardens , have described them as distinct
species.

The bark of the Black Walnut is thick, blackish, and
on old trees deeply furrowed. When the timber is
freshly cut, the sap is white and the heart of a violet
colour, which after a short exposure to the air assumes
an intenser shade, and becomes nearly black : hence
probably is derived the name of Black Walnut. There
are several qualities for which its wood is principally
esteemed ; it remains sound during a long time, even
when exposed to the influences of heat and moisture;
but this observation is applicable only to the heart, the
sap speedily decays : it is very strong and very tenacious :
when thoroughly seasoned it is not liable to warp and
split; and its grain is sufficiently fine and compact to
admit of a beautiful polish. It possesses in addition to
these advantages, that of being secure from worms.
On account of these excellencies, it is preferred and
successfully employed in many kinds of work. East of
the Alleghanies, its timber is not extensively used in
building houses, but in some parts of Kentucky and Ohio,
it is split into shingles 18 inches long and from 4 to 6
inches wide, which serve to cover them : sometimes
also this timber enters into the composition of the frame.
But it is chiefly in cabinet making, that the Black Walnut
is employed wherever it abounds. By selecting pieces from
the upper part of the trunk, immediately below the
first ramification, furniture is sometimes made, which
from the accidental curlings of the grain is highly beautiful; but as its colour soon changes to a dusky hue, the

Wild Cherry wood is frequently preferred for this use. The Black Walnut is also employed for the stocks of military muskets; it is stronger and tougher than the Red flowering Maple, which, from its superior lightness and elegance, is chosen for fowling pieces. In Virginia posts are very commonly made of Black Walnut, and as it lasts undecayed in the ground from 20 to 25 years, it appears every way fit for this purpose. I have been assured that it makes excellent naves for wheels, which farther proves its strength and durability. At Philadelphia, coffins are universally made of it.

The timber of this tree is also excellently adapted to certain uses in Naval Architecture. It should never be wrought till it is perfectly seasoned, after which it is asserted to be more durable, though more brittle, than the White Oak. Breckel in his history of North Carolina, affirms that it is not liable, like the Oak, to be attacked by sea-worms in warm latitudes. This advantage if it is real, is highly important, and deserves to be ascertained by farther observation. In the marine lumber yards of Philadelphia, I have often seen it used for knees and floor timber; but in the vessels built at Wheeling and Marietta, small towns on the Ohio, it constitutes a principal part of the frame. On the river Wabash, canoes are made of it which are greatly esteemed for strength and durability. Some of them fashioned from the trunk of a single tree, are more than 40 feet long, and 2 or 3 feet wide.

The Black Walnut is exported in small quantities to England in planks of 2 inches in thickness. These planks are sold at Philadelphia, at four cents a foot.

The husk of the fruit yields a colour similar to that which is obtained from the European Walnut. It is used in the country for dying woolen stuffs.

This tree has been long since introduced, in England and France, into the gardens of the lovers of foreign culture. It succeeds perfectly and yields fruit abundantly. Though differing widely from the European species, it bears a nearer resemblance to it than any other American Walnut. By comparing the two species as to their utility in the arts and in commerce, it will appear, that the wood of the Black Walnut is more compact, heavier and much stronger; that it is susceptible of a finer polish, and that it is not injured by worms; qualities which, as has been seen, render it fit not only for the same uses with ours, but also for the larger works of architecture. These considerations sufficiently evince that it is a valuable tree, and that it is with great reason, that many proprietors in America have spared it, in clearing their new lands. On high roads, I am of opinion that it might be chosen to succeed the Elm; for experience has proved, that to insure success in the continued cultivation of trees or herbaceous plants on the same soil, the practice must be varied with species of different genera.

Nuts of the European Walnut and of the Black Walnut

have been planted at the same time in the same soil; those of the Black Walnut are observed to shoot more vigorously, and to grow in a given time to a greater height. By grafting the European upon the American species, at the height of 8 or 10 feet, their advantages, with respect to the quality both of wood and of fruit, might be united.

PLATE XXX.

A leaf of half its natural size. Fig. 1, A nut with its huk. Fig. 2, A nut without its husk. Fig. 3, A barren ament.

BUTTERNUT.

Juglans cathartica. J. foliolis subquindenis, lanceolatis, basi rotundato-obtusis, subtùs tomentosis, leviter serratis: fructu oblongo, ovato, apice rimoso, viscido, longè pedunculato, nuce oblongâ, acuminatâ, insigniter insculptâ scabrosa.

THIS species of Walnut is known in North America, under different denominations. In Massachusetts, New Hampshire, and Vermont, it bears the name of Oil nut; in Pennsylvania and Maryland, and on the banks of the Ohio, it is generally known by that of White Walnut; in Connecticut, New York, New Jersey, Virginia, and in the mountainous districts of the upper parts of the Carolinas, it is called Butternut. The last of these names I have retained, because it is not wholly unknown in those parts of the United States where the others are in general use, and because the wood is employed in the neighbourhood of New York, for a greater variety of uses than elsewhere. I think also that the latin specific name *Cathartica*, which was long since given it by Doctor Cutler of Massachusetts, should be definitively substituted for that of *Cinerea*, by which it has hitherto been distinguished among Botanists. This last appellation, derived from the colour of the secondary branches, whose bark is smooth and greyish, suggests only an unimportant characteristic,

Pl. 31

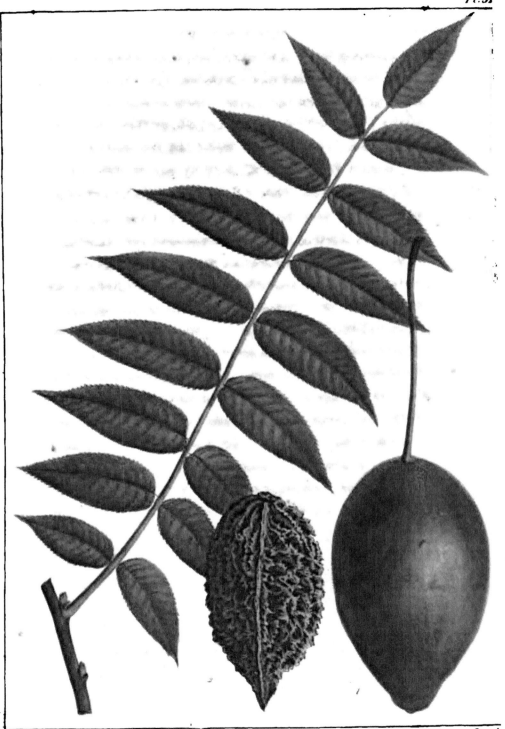

P J Redouté del.

Renard

Butter Nut.

Juglans cathartica.

while the first expresses one of the most interesting properties of the tree.

The Butternut is found in Upper and Lower Canada, in the District of Maine, on the shores of Lake Erie, in the States of Kentucky and Tennessee and on the banks of the Missouri; but I have never met with it in the lower parts of the Carolinas, of Georgia, and of East Florida, where the nature of the soil and the intemperate heat of the summer, are unfavorable to its vegetation. In cold regions, on the contrary, its growth is luxuriant; for in the State of Vermont, where the winter is so rigorous that sledges are used during four months in the year, this tree attains a circumference of 8 or 10 feet. I have nowhere seen it more abundant, than in the bottoms which border the Ohio between Wheeling and Marietta : but the thickness of these forests, which are hardly penetrated by the sun, appears to prevent its utmost expansion. I have seen here no trees as large as some in New Jersey, on the steep and elevated banks of the Hudson, nearly opposite to the city of New York. The woods in this place are thin, and the soil cold, unproductive, and interspersed with large rocks, in the interstices of which the biggest Butternuts have their root. I have measured some of them, which at 5 feet from the ground, were 10 or 12 feet in circumference, and which were 50 feet in height, with roots extending even with the surface of the ground, in a serpentine direction, and with little variation in size, to the distance of 40 feet. The trunk ramifies at a small height, and the branches seeking a direction more horizontal than those of other trees , and spreading widely, form a large and tufted head , which gives the tree a remarkable appearance.

The buds of the Butternut , like those of the Black Walnut, are uncovered. In the spring its vegetation is forward, and its leaves unfold a fortnight earlier than those of the Hickories. Each leaf is composed of 7 or 8 pair of sessile leaflets, and terminated by a petiolated odd one. The leaflets are from 2 to 3 inches in length , lanceolate, serrate, and slightly downy. The barren flowers stand on large cylindrical aments , which are single, 4 or 5 inches long, and attached to the shoots of the preceding year; the fertile flowers on the contrary, come out on the shoots of the same spring, and are situated at their extremity. The ovarium is crowned by two rose coloured stigmata. The fruit is commonly single, and suspended by a thin , pliable peduncle, about 3 inches in length ; its form is oblong-oval without any appearance of seam.It is often 2 inches and a half in length, and 5 inches in circumference, and is covered with a viscid adhesive substance , composed of small transparent vesicles , which are easily discerned with the aid of a glass. The nuts are hard , oblong , rounded at the base , and terminated at the summit, in an acute point; the surface is very rough , and deeply and irregularly furrowed. They are ripe , in the neighbourhood of New

York, about the 15ᵗʰ of september, a fortnight earlier than the other species of Walnut. Some years they are so abundant, that one person may gather several bushels of them in a day. The kernel is thick and oily, and soon becomes rancid; hence, doubtless, are derived the names of Butternut and Oilnut. These nuts are rarely seen in the markets of New York and Philadelphia. The Indians who inhabited these regions, pounded and boiled them, and separating the oily substance which swam upon the surface, mixed it with their food: When the fruit has attained about half its growth, it is sometimes used for making pickles, being first plunged into boiling water, and thoroughly wiped, to clean it of its down, and afterwards preserved in vinegar.

The Black Walnut and Butternut, when young, resemble each other in their foliage, and in the rapidity of their growth; but when arrived at maturity, their forms are so different, as to be distinguishable at first sight. Remarkable peculiarities are also found, on examining their wood, especially when seasoned; the Black Walnut is heavy, strong, and of a dark brown colour; while the Butternut is light, of little strength, and of a reddish hue : but they possess in common, the great advantage of lasting long, and of being secure from the annoyance of worms. From its want of solidity and from the difficulty of procuring pieces of considerable length, Butternut timber is never used in the cities, in the construction of houses, though it is sometimes employed for this purpose in the country. In some Districts of New Jersey, it is often taken for the sleepers which are placed immediately on the ground, in the framing of houses and barns. As it long resists the effects of heat and moisture, it is esteemed for the posts and rails of rural fence, and for troughs for the use of cattle. For corn shovels and wooden dishes, it is preferred to the Red flowering Maple, because it is lighter and less liable to split; consequently articles made of it, are sold at a higher price. Near New-York, I have observed it to be made use of for canoes formed of one or two logs, and for the futtocks destined to give them solidity; but in boats of considerable size some stronger wood is selected for this purpose. At Pittsburgh on the Ohio, the Butternut is sometimes sawn into planks, for the construction of small skiffs, which, on account of their lightness, are in request for descending the river. At Windsor in Vermont, it is used for the pannels of coaches and chaises; the workmen find it excellently adapted to this object, not only from its lightness, but because it is not liable to split, and receives paint in a superior manner : indeed I have remarked that its pores are more open than those of the Poplar and Basswood.

The medicinal properties of Butternut bark, have long since been proved, by several eminent Physicians of the United States, and among others, by Doctor Cutler. An extract in water, or even a decoction sweet-

ened with honey, is acknowledged to be one of the best
cathartics afforded by *materia medica;* its purgative
operation is always sure, and unattended, in the most
delicate constitutions, with pain or irritation. Experience
has shewn that it produces the best effects in many
cases of dysentery. It is commonly given in the form
of pills, and to adults, in doses from half a dram to
a dram. It is not however in general use, except
in the country, where many of the farmers wives
provide a small store of it in the spring, for the wants
of their families and of their neighbours. They obtain
it by boiling the bark entire in water, till the liquid is
reduced by evaporation, to a thick, viscid substance,
which is almost black. This is a faulty process; the
exterior bark, or the dead part which covers the
cellular integument, should first be taken off, for by
continued boiling, it becomes charged with four fifths of
the liquid, already enriched with extractive matter. I
have also seen this bark successfully employed as a re-
vulsive, in inflammatory ophthalmias and in the tooth-
ache : a piece of it soaked in warm water is applied in
these cases to the back of the neck. In the country it is
sometimes employed for dying wool of a dark brown
colour ; but the bark of the Black Walnut is preferable
for this purpose.

On a live tree, the cellular integument, when first exposed, is of a pure white, in a moment, it changes to a
beautiful lemon colour, and soon after to a deep brown.

If the trunk of the Butternut is pierced in the month which precedes the unfolding of the leaves , a pretty copious discharge ensues of a slightly sugary sap , from which , by evaporation , sugar is obtained of a quality inferior to that of the Sugar Maple.

Although the Butternut, as has been seen , possesses useful properties , I do not think it sufficiently valuable , either in the arts , or for fuel , to recommend its introduction into the forests of the old continent : it should find place only in our pleasure grounds.

PLATE XXXI.

A leaf of half its natural size. Fig. 1 , A nut with its husk. Fig. 2 , A nut without its husk.

Pl. 32.

Pacanenut Hickory.
Juglans olivæ-formis.

PACANENUT HICKORY.

JUGLANS OLIVÆFORMIS. J. *foliolis plurimis, subpetiolatis, falcatis, serratis; fructu oblongo, prominulo-quadran-gulo; nuce olivæformi, levi.*

THIS species, which is found in upper Louisiana, is called by the French of Illinois and New Orleans, *Paca-nier*, and its fruit *Pacanes*. This name has been adopted by the inhabitants of the United States, who call it Pa-canenut. On the borders of the rivers Missouri, Illinois, St.-Francis, and Arkansas, it is most abundantly multi-plied; it is also common on the river Wabash; on the Ohio, it is found for 200 miles from its junction with the Mississippi : higher than this, it becomes more rare, and is not seen beyond Louisville. My father, in traver-sing this country, learned from the French inhabit-ants, who ascend the Mississippi in quest of furs, that it is not found on that river, beyond the mouth of the Great Mackakity, which discharges itself in the la-titude of 42° 51′.

This tree grows most naturally, in cold and wet grounds. There is a swamp of 800 acres, situated on the right bank of the Ohio, oppositite to the river Cumber-land, which is said to be entirely covered with it, and which is called by the French, *la pacanière*.

The Pacanenut is a beautiful tree, with a straight and

well shaped trunk ; in the forests it reaches the height of
60 or 70 feet. Its wood is coarse grained, and like the
other Hickories, heavy and compact : it possesses also
great strength and durability ; but in these respects, it
is inferior to some species which remain to be described.
Its buds, like those of the Black Walnut, and Butternut
are uncovered. The leaves are from 12 to 18 inches in
length, and are supported by petioles some what angular, and slightly downy in the spring. Each leaf is composed of 6 or 7 pair of sessile leaflets, and terminated
by a petiolated odd one, which is commonly smaller than the pair immediately preceding. The leaflets,
on flourishing trees, are from 2 to 3 inches long, ovate,
serrate, and remarkable for the circular form of the
upper edge, while the lower one is less rounded. It is
also to be noticed, that the main rib is placed a little below the middle of the leaflet.

The nuts, which are usually abundant, are contained
in a husk from 1 to 2 lines thick, and have four
slightly prominent angles, corresponding to their internal
divisions. They vary in length from an inch to an inch and a
half, are pointed at the extremities, of a cylindrical form,
and of a yellowish colour marked, at the period of perfect maturity, with blackish or purple lines. The shell is
smooth and thin, though too hard to be broken by the
fingers : the kernel is full, and not being divided by
ligneous partitions, is easily extracted. These nuts,
which are of a very agreeable taste, form an object of

petty commerce, between Upper and Lower Louisiana. From New Orleans, they are exported to the West Indies, and to the ports of the United States. They are not only better than any other species of North American walnuts, but they appear to me to be more delicately flavoured than those of Europe. And besides, varieties of the Pacanenut are found, whose fruit is far superior to that of the European Walnut unimproved by culture. I am opinion then, that this tree merits the attention both of Americans and Europeans, and that by assiduous cultivation, it may be brought to a high degree of perfection. These advantages, it is true, are balanced in part by the slowness of its growth; there are trees in France which have been planted more than thirty years, and which do not yield fruit.

If the practise should be successfully adopted, of grafting the Pacanenut on the Black Walnut, or on the Common Walnut, its vegetation would be incomparably more rapid, and no motive would discourage its propagation in Europe.

PLATE XXXII.

A leaf of half its natural size. Fig. 2, *A nut with its husk. Fig.* 2, *A nut without its husk.*

BITTERNUT HICKORY.

Juglans amara. J. *arbor maxima, foliolis* 7—9ⁿⁱˢ, *glabris, conspicuè serratis, impari breviter petiolato : fructu sub-rotundo-ovoideo, supernè suturis prominulis; nuce levi, subglobosâ, mucronatâ : putamine fragili, nucleo amaro.*

This species is generally known in New Jersey by the name of Bitternut Hickory; in Pennsylvania, and particularly in the county of Lancaster, it is called White Hickory and sometimes Swamp Hickory; farther south, it is confounded with the Pignut Hickory; the French of Illinois, like the inhabitants of New Jersey, give it the name of Bitternut, which, as it indicates one of the peculiar properties of the fruit, I have chosen to retain.

The Bitternut Hickory, I believe, is nowhere found much beyond the boundaries of Vermont, in the latitude of 45°. It is not seen in the Province of Maine, where the borders of the rivers offer situations, analogous to those in which it abounds, a few degrees farther south. In Bergen woods, six miles from New-York, and in the bottoms which stretch along the Ohio, it grows to a very lofty stature; I have measured trees which were 10 or 12 feet in circumference, and 70 or 80 feet high. It attains these dimensions, only in spots where the soil is excellent, constantly cool, and often inundated by creeks and rivers. It is probably because it thrives most in such situations.

Pl.3

H Redouté del.

Cally sc.

Bitter Nut Hickory.

Juglans amara.

that it is sometimes called Swamp Hickory. Of all the Hickories the vegetation of this species is the latest ; I have uniformly observed, that its leaves unfold a fortnight after the others. On flourishing trees at an age to bear fruit, they are 12 or 15 inches in length and nearly as much in breadth ; the size, as in other vegetables, varies according to the nature of the soil, and the situation of the leaf upon a lower or upon an upper branch. Each leaf is composed of 3 or 4 pair of leaflets, and terminated by an odd one, which is larger than the preceding pair. The leaflets are about 6 inches in length, and an inch in breadth, sessile, oval-acuminate, deeply toothed, smooth, and of a pretty dark green. When the tree has shed its leaves, it may still be distinguished by its yellow and naked buds.

In Pennsylvania and New Jersey, the Bitternut Hickory blossoms about the 25th of May. The peduncles of the barren flowers are in pairs, each supporting three flexible and pendulous aments : they are attached at the basis of the shoots of the same season, while the fertile aments, which are not conspicuous, are placed at the extremity.

The fruit is ripe about the beginning of October ; it is so plentiful that several bushels are sometimes gathered from a single tree. The husk is thin, fleshy, and surmounted on its upper half by four appendages in the form of wings. It never becomes ligneous, like those of the other Hickories, but softens and decays. The

form of the nut in this species is more constant and
more regular than in the others. It is broader than it is
long, being 6 or 7 lines one way and 10 lines the other.
The shell is white, smooth, and thin enough to be
broken by the fingers. The kernel is remarkable for the
deep inequalities produced on every side by its fol-
dings. It is so harsh and bitter, that squirrels and other
wild animals will not feed on it, while any other nut
is to be found.

In some parts of Pennsylvania where this tree is
multiplied, an oil is extracted from the nuts, which
is used for the lamp and for other inferior purposes.
But from these experiments, in which individuals have
succeeded, it is not to be concluded that a sufficient
product of this sort can be obtained to form a branch
of industry ; neither this, nor any other species of
Walnut, is abundant enough in the United States.

In the texture of its bark, and in the colour of its
heart and sap, the Bitternut Hickory resembles the
other Hickories, and its wood possesses, though in
an inferior degree, the weight, strength, tenacity,
and elasticity, which so plainly distinguish them. At
Lancaster, it is used for fuel, but it is not considered superior to the White Oak, nor sold at a higher
price.

The Bitternut Hickory exists and bears fruit in several gardens in France ; but as it is of no value for its
nuts, and flourishes only in very fertile soils ; as its

wood, also, is proved in America to be inferior to that of the following species, I think it should not be propagated in the forests of Europe.

PLATE XXXIII.

A leaf of its natural size. Fig. 1, A nut with its husk. Fig. 2, A nut without its husk.

WATER BITTERNUT HICKORY.

Juglans aquatica. J. foliolis 9—11*nis*, *lanceolato-acumi-
natis*, *subserratis*, *sessillibus*, *impari breviter petiolato:
fructibus pedunculatis*, *nuce subdepressâ, parvâ, rubigi-
nosâ, tenerâ.*

No specific name has hitherto been given to this species, which is confined to the Southern States; it is confounded with the Pignut Hickory, though differing from
it in many respects. The name which I propose, appears
sufficiently appropriate, for I have always found this
tree in swamps, and in the ditches which surround
the rice fields, where it is accompanied by the Red
flowering Maple, Tupelo, Cypress, and Carolina Poplar. The Water Bitternut Hickory grows to the height
of 40 or 50 feet, and in its general appearance, resembles the other Hickories. Its leaves are 8 or 9 inches long,
and of a beautiful green. They are composed of 4 or 5
pair of sessile leaflets surmounted by a petiolated odd
one. The leaflets are serrate, 4 or 5 inches long, 8 or 9
lines broad, and very similar to the leaves of the
Peach tree.

The husk is thin, and the nuts are small, angular,
a little depressed at the sides, somewhat rough, of a
reddish colour, and very tender. The kernel is formed
in folds like that of the Bitternut Hickory: as may be
supposed, it is not eatable. The wood of this species,

Pl. 34.

Water bitter Nut Hickory.

Juglans aquatica.

though partaking of the common properties of the Hickories, is in every respect inferior to the others, from the nature of the grounds on which it grows.

The Water Bitternut Hickory , which I have introduced into France, flourishes unchecked by the rigours of our Winters ; but I do not think it deserves to find a place , in the forests of Europe , nor to be spared in clearing the new lands of America. The southern parts of the United States possess many sorts of timber more useful in building , to which purpose this, like the other Hickories , is poorly adapted.

PLATE XXXIV.

A branch with leaves of the natural size. Fig. 1 , Nuts with their husks. Fig. 2 , Nuts without their husks.

MOCKERNUT HICKORY.

JUGLANS TOMENTOSA. J. *foliolis* 7—9^{nis}, *leviter serratis, conspicuè villosis, impari subpetiolato : amentis compositis, longissimis, filiformibus, eximiè tomentosis: fructu globoso vel oblongo; nuce quadranguld, crassd, durissimdque.*

IN the parts of New Jersey which lie on the river Hudson, and in the City of New York and its vicinity, this species is known by the name of Mockernut Hickory, and less commonly of White heart Hickory; at Philadelphia and Baltimore, and in Virginia, that of Common Hickory is the only one in use. The French of Illinois call it *Noyer dur*, or Hard Walnut. The first of these denominations, which is descriptive of the fruit, I have for that reason adopted.

This species is not, as the name which it bears it that country would indicate, more multiplied in Pennsylvania, and farther south, than the other Hickories. I have not seen it north of Portsmouth in New Hampshire, though 100 miles south in the neighbourhood of Boston and Providence, it is common. It is most abundant in the forests that still remain on the coast of the middle States, and in those which cover the Upper parts of the Carolinas and of Georgia; but in the last mentioned states, it becomes more rare in ap-

Pl.35.

Mocker Nut Hickory.

proaching the sea, as the sterility of the soil, in general dry and sandy, is unpropitious to its growth. I have noticed, however, that this is the only Hickory which springs in the Pine Barrens : the sprouts are burnt every year, and never rise higher than 3 or 4 feet. I have made the same observation, in traversing the Big Barrens of Kentucky and Tennessee, where the Mockernut Hickory and Black Jack Oak alone are seen. They survive the conflagrations, which almost every spring envelop the *prairies*, but their vegetation is checked by the fire, and they do not exceed the height of 8 or 10 feet.

Like most of the Walnuts, the Mockernut Hickory flourishes in rich soils, and chiefly on the gentle acclivities which surround the swamps, where it grows, mingled with the Sweet Gum, Poplar, Sugar Maple, Bitternut Hickory, and Black Walnut. In these situations it reaches its greatest size, which is commonly about 60 feet in height, and 18 or 20 inches in diameter. I remember to have seen larger Mockernut Hickories near Lexington in Kentucky, but this extraordinary growth in several species of trees, is rarely seen on this side of the Alleghanies, and is attributable to the extreme fertility of the soil in the Western Country. Of all the Hickories, however, the Mockernut succeeds best on lands of a middling quality ; for it for forms a part of the waste and impoverished forests, which cover the meager sandy soil of Lower

Virginia ; though under these disadvantages it exhibits but a mean and stunted appearance.

The buds of this species are large , short, of a greyish white, and very hard; in the winter, after the falling of the leaf, they afford the only characteristic by which the tree can be distinguished , when it exceeds 8 or 10 feet in height. It the beginning of May, the buds swell, the external scales fall off, and the inner ones soon after burst and display the young leaf. The leaves grow so rapidly that I have seen them gain 20 inches in eighteen days. They are composed of 4 pair of sessile leaflets , and terminated by an odd one. The leaflets are large oval-acuminate, serrate, pretty thick, and hairy underneath , as is also the common petiole to which they are attached. With the first frosts, the leaves change to a beautiful yellow, and fall soon after. The barren flowers appear on pendulous , downy, axillary aments , 6 or 8 inches long; the fertile flowers, which are not very conspicuous, are of a pale rose colour, and are situated at the extremity of the young shoots.

The fruit is ripe about the 15th of November. It is odorous, sessile or rarely pedunculated, and commonly united in pairs. In form and size , it exhibits remarkable varieties : on some trees it is round, with depressed seams, on others oblong, with angular or prominent seams; it is sometimes 2 inches long and 12 or 15 lines in diameter, and sometimes of less than half this size. It differs also in weight, as well as in configuration and

volume, varying from one dram to four. The largest
nuts, might be confounded with those of the Thick
Shellbark Hickory, and the smallest, with those of the
Pignut Hickory: I have selected for the drawing a nut of
the most common size. The shell is very thick, somewhat channeled, and extremely hard. The kernel is
sweet but minute, and difficult to extract, on account
of the strong partitions which divide it : hence, probably, is derived the name of Mockernut, and hence
also, this fruit is rarely seen in the markets.

The trunk of the old Mockernut Hickory is covered
with a thick, hard, and rugged bark. Its wood is of
the same colour and texture, with the other Hickories,
and characterised by the qualities which render this
class of trees so remarkable. It is particularly esteemed
for fuel, for which use, trees of 6 or 8 inches in
diameter are preferred. At this stage of its growth,
while the heart, the proper colour of which is reddish
is not yet developped, it frequently goes by the name
of White heart Hickory. In the country, a greenish
colour is sometimes extracted from the bark, but it is
not extensively in use.

Of all the Hickories, this species is of the slowest
growth : a fact which I have proved by planting nuts
of the several species, and by comparing the length of
their annual shoots. I have also been led to believe,
that it is the most liable to be attacked by worms, and
especially by the *Callidium flexuosum*, whose larva eats

within the body of the tree. These considerations appears sufficiently weighty, to induce cultivators, in forming large plantations , to prefer some of the species
which are described in the sequel.

PLATE XXXV.

*A leaf of a third of its natural size. Fig. 1, A nut with
its husk. Fig. 2, A nut without its husk. Fig. 3, Callidium
flexuosum.*

Pl. 36

Shell bark Hickory.

Juglans squamosa.

SHELLBARK HICKORY.

JUGLANS SQUAMOSA. J. *foliolis quinis , majoribus , longè petiolatis , ovato-acuminatis , serratis , subtùs villosis , impari sessili ; amentis masculis , compositis , glabris , filiformibus : fructu globoso , depresso , majore ; nuce compressâ , albâ.*

THE singular disposition of the bark , in this species, has given rise to the descriptive names of Shellbark , Shagbark, and Scalybark Hickory , the first of which as being most generally in use in the middle and southern states, I have adopted. Many descendants of the Dutch settlers , who inhabit the parts of the of New Jersey near the city of New York, call it *Kisky Thomas nut*, and the French of Illinois, know it by the name of *Noyer tendre*, or Soft Walnut.

Beyond Portsmouth in New Hampshire, I have not observed the Shell bark Hickory; and even there, its vegetation being impeded by the rigours of the climate , its stature is low, and its fruit small. I have not found it in the forests of the District of Maine, nor in those of Vermont, situated a little higher towards the North. It abounds on the shores of Lake Erie , about Geneva in Genesee, along the Mohawk river, in the neighbourhood of Goshen in New Jersey, and on the banks of the Susquehannah and Schuylkill rivers in Pennsylva-

nia. In Maryland, in the lower parts of Virginia, and
in the other southern states it is less common. In South
Carolina, I have nor noticed it nearer Charleston
than the parish of Goose-Creek about 24 miles distant. It
is met with in the Western States, but not as frequently as the following species, the Thick Shellbark Hickory, to which it bears a striking analogy, and with
which it is confounded by the inhabitants. East of the
Alleghanies, the Shellbark Hickory grows almost exclusively about swamps and wet grounds, which are
exposed to be inundated for several weeks together: in
these situations, it is found in company with the
Swamp White Oak, Red flowering Maple, Sweet Gum,
Buttonwood and Tupelo. Of all the Hickories, this species grows to the greatest height with proportionally
the smallest diameter, for it is sometimes seen 80 or
90 feet high, and less than 2 feet thick. The trunk is
destitute of branches, regularly shaped, and of an almost uniform size for three quarters of its length, thus
forming a very fine tree. The greatest peculiarity in its
appearance, and that by which it is most easily distinguished, is the surface of the trunk. The exterior bark
is divided into a great number of long, narrow plates,
which bend outwards at the ends, and adhere only in
the middle. Bristling in this manner with projecting
points, the Shellbark Hickory attracts the attention of
the most careless observer. This remarkable exfoliation
of the epidermis takes place, only in trees which

exceed 10 inches in diameter, though it is much earlier
indicated by seams. This characteristic, by which the
tree may be recognised in winter when stript of its
leaves, does not exist during the 7 or 8 first years of
its growth; and during this period, it may easily be
confounded with the Mockernut Hickory and Pignut
Hickory, if recourse is not had to the buds. In these
two species, and generally in all trees, the buds are
formed of scales closely applied one upon another; in
the species which we are considering, the two external
scales adhere for only half the length of the bud, and
leave the upper part uncovered. I allow myself the conjecture, that in this disposition of the scales, which is
peculiar to this and the following species, should be
sought the origin of the exfoliation of the bark. When
the sap begins to ascend in the spring, the outer scales
fall, and the inner ones swell and become covered
with a yellowish silky down : after a fortnight, the
buds, which are already 2 inches long, open and give
birth to the young leaves. The growth of the leaves
is so rapid, that in a month they attain their full length,
which on young and vigorous trees, is sometimes 20
inches. They consist of 2 pair of leaflets with a ses-
sil odd one. The leaflets are very large, oval-acuminate, serrate, and slightly downy underneath. The
barren flowers, which in the State of New York appear
from the 15th to the 20th of May, are disposed as in the
preceding species, on long, glabrous, filiform, pen-

dulous aments, of which three are united on a common petiole, attached at the basis of the young shoots; the fertile flowers, of a greenish hue and scarcely apparent, are situated at the extremity. The fruit of the Shellbark Hickory is ripe about the beginning of October. Some years it is so abundant, that several bushels may be gathered from a single tree. It varies in size, according to the soil and the exposure in which it is produced, but five inches and a half may be assumed as the average of its circumference. The shape is uniformly round, with four depressed seams, in which the husk opens at the season of perfect maturity, dividing itself completly into equal sections. The entire separation of the husk, and its thickness disproportioned to the size of the nut, form a character peculiar to the Shellbark Hickories. The nuts of this species are small, white, compressed at the sides, and marked by four distinct angles, which correspond to the divisions of the husk.

The Shellbark nut contains a fuller and sweeter kernel than any American Walnut, except the Pacane-nut. The shell, though thin, must be cracked before being brought upon the table, as it is too hard to be crushed in the fingers like the European Walnut, which is certainly a superior fruit. These nuts are in such request, that they form a small article of commerce, registered on the list of exports of the products of the United States. This exportation, which does not exceed four of five hundred bushels annually, takes place from New York and from the small ports of Connecticut, to the Southern States, to the West India Islands, and even to Liverpool ; where the fruit is known by the name of Hickory nuts. In the market of New York, they are sold at two dollars a bushel. They are gathered in the forests, and from insulated trees, which, in some places, have been spared in clearing the lands : a precaution which I have particularly noticed to have been used near Goshen in New Jersey, and on several estates about 30 miles beyond Albany.

The Indians who inhabit the Shores of Lake Erie and Lake Michigan, lay up a store of these nuts for the winter, a part of which they pound in wooden mortars, and boiling the paste in water, collect the oily matter which swims upon the surface, to season their aliments.

Before speaking of the properties of the wood, I cannot forbear mentioning a fine variety of Shellbark nuts, produced upon a farm at Seacocus, near Shakehill in New Jersey. They are nearly twice as large as any that I have seen elsewhere, and have a white shell with rounded prominences instead of angles. A century of cultivation, perhaps, would not advance the species generally to an equal degree of perfection ;

and probably this variety might still be improved by grafting.

The wood of the Shellbark Hickory possesses all the characteristic properties of the Hickories, being strong, elastic and tenacious. It has also their common defects of soon decaying and of being eaten by worms. As this tree stretches up to a great height with nearly an uniform diameter, it is sometimes employed at New York and Philadelphia for the keels of vessels; but it is now seldom used for this purpose, most of the large trees near the sea ports being already consumed. Its wood is found to split most easily and to be the most elastic; for this reason it is used for making baskets, and also for whip-handles which are esteemed for their suppleness; several cases of them are annually exported to England. For the same excellence, and for the superior fineness of its grain it is selected, in the neighbourhood of New York and Philadelphia, for the back-bows of Windsor chairs, which are wholly of wood. I have frequently observed that among the Hickory wood brought to New York for fuel, this species predominated.

Such are the uses to which the Shellbark Hickory appears peculiarly adapted. It has before been seen to be a tree of lofty stature and of majestic appearance : I should therefore recommend its introduction into the European forests, where it should be con-

signed to cool and humid places, congenial with those
in which it flourishes in America. In the North of
Europe it could not fail of succeeding, as it securely
braves the extremest cold.

PLATE XXXVI.

*Fig. 1, A nut with its husk. Fig. 2, A section of the husk.
Fig. 3, A nut without its husk. Fig. 3, A barren ament divided into three parts.*

THICK SHELLBARK HICKORY.

JUGLANS LACINIOSA. J. *foliis majoribus, q—g^{nk}, ovato-acuminatis, serratis, subtomentosis, impari, petiolato: fructu majore, ovato; nuce oblongâ, crassâ, mediocriter compressâ.*

THIS species bears a striking analogy to the preceding, and is frequently confounded with it by the inhabitants of the Western Country : some of them distinguish it by the name of Thick Shellbark Hickory, which should be preserved as its appropriate denomination. East of the Alleghanies this tree is rare, and is found only in a few places ; it grows on the Schuylkill river 30 or 40 miles from its junction with the Delaware, and in the vicinity of Springfield 15 or 20 miles from Philadelphia, where its fruit is called Springfield nut. It is also found in Glocester County, in Virginia, under the name of Glocester Walnut. These different denominations confirm my observation, that this species is little multiplied on the eastern side of the Alleghany mountains ; a fact of which I became assured in travelling through the country. It abounds, on the other hand, in the bottoms which skirt the Ohio and the rivers which empty into it, where it unites with the Honey Locust, Black Maple, Hackberry, Black Walnut, Wild Cherry, White and Red Elm, Box Elder, White Maple,

Pl. 37.

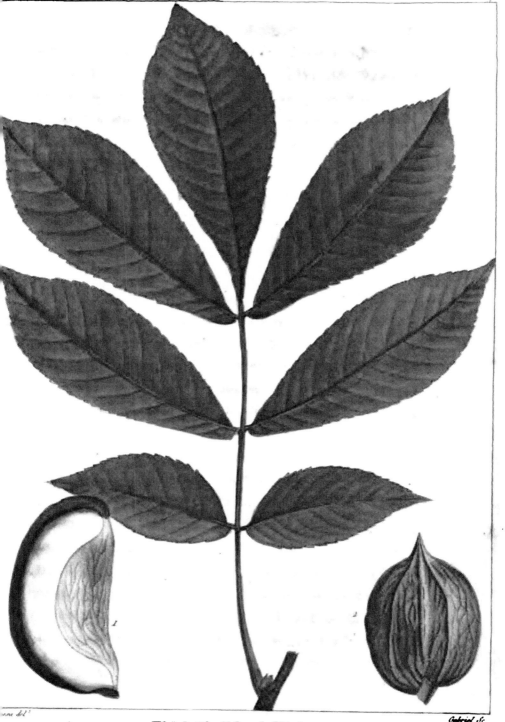

Thick Shell bark Hickory.

Juglans laciniosa.

and Button wood, to form the thick and gloomy forests
which cover these vallies. Like the Shellbark Hickory it
grows to the height of 80 feet, and its ample head is
supported by a straight trunk, in diameter, proportioned to its elevation. The bark exhibits the same singular
arrangement with that of the Shellbark Hickory ;
it is divided into strips from 1 to 3 feet long, which
are warped outwards at the end, and attached only in
the middle. They fall and are succeeded by others similarly disposed. It is only observable that in this species the plates are narrower, more numerous, and of
a lighter colour; from which differences, I have thought
proper to give it the specific name of *laciniosa*. The
outer scales of the buds do not adhere entirely to the
inner ones, but retire as in the Shellbark Hickory. The
leaves also, which vary in length from 8 to 20 inches,
observe the same process in unfolding, and are similar
in size, configuration, and texture; but they differ in
being composed of seven leaflets, and sometimes
of nine instead of five, the invariable number of the
Shellbark Hickory. The barren aments are disposed in
the same form, though they are, perhaps, a little longer than in the other species. The fertile flowers appear, not very conspicuously, at the extremity of the
shoots of the same spring. They are succeeded by a
large oval fruit, more than 2 inches long, and 4 or 5
inches in circumference. Like that of the Shellbark
Hickory, it has four depressed seams, which at its com-

plete maturity, open through their whole length for the
escape of the nut. The nut of this species is widely different from the other; it is nearly twice as big, it is
longer than it is broad, and is terminated at each end in
a firm point. The shell is also thicker and of a yellowish hue, while that of the Shellbark nut is white.

From the colour of its nut, the Shellbark Hickory received the specific name of *alba*, which I have changed,
as it indicates a character possessed by it in common
with another species, found in the Royal gardens of
the *Petit Trianon*. This species, originally from North
America, belongs to the Scalybark Hickories. The nuts
are white, and the entire fruit, though a little inferior
in size, resembles that of the proper Shellbark Hickory.
By its foliage, it is related to the Thick Shellbark Hickory, each leaf being composed of 4 pair of leaflets
with an odd one. The specific name of *ambigua*, might
with propriety be given to it.

The nuts of the Thick Shellbark Hickory are brought
every autumn to the market of Philadelphia, but the quantity does not exceed a few bushels, and they are generally
sold mixed with those of the Mockernut Hickory, which
resemble some varieties of this species. The Glocester Hickory I consider only as a variety of the Thick Shellbark
Hickory, to which it bears the strongest likeness in its appearance, in its young shoots, in the number of its
leaflets, and in its barren aments. The only essential
difference is in the nuts; those of the Glocester Walnut

are a third larger, with the shell one half thicker, and
so hard that it requires pretty heavy blows of a hammer
to crack them. In colour, they resemble the nuts of the
Mockernut Hickory, with the finest varieties of which,
they might from this circumstance be confounded.

The Thick Shellbark Hickory, as has been said, is
nearly related to the Shellbark Hickory, and its wood,
which is of the same colour and texture, unites the
peculiar qualities of that species, with such as are
common to the Hickories. Its fruit, though larger, is
inferior in taste and this consideration should induce proprietors in the Western Country, in clearing their new
lands, to spare the true Shellbark Hickory in preference, when both species are found upon the same
soil. For the same reason, and for its favourable growth
in less fertile grounds, and even in elevated situations,
a fact which I have observed near Brownsville on the
Alleghany river, the same preference should, I think,
be given to it in the forests of Europe.

In the description of the Scaly bark Hickories it has
been seen, that they exhibit many striking traits of resemblance, which may warrant the grouping of them
into a secondary section. Besides their generic and
specific characters, they possess others peculiar to
themselves, by which they are so nearly related, that
were it not for some remarkable differences, they might
be treated as a single species. The general characters
of the Hickories are, three-clefted, pliable, and pen-

dulous barren aments, and certain common properties of the wood. To these are added in the Scaly Hickories, a very thick husk covering the nut completely,
and divided into four parts when ripe; a shaggy bark
on the trunk, indicated, in my opinion, by the
external scales of the buds not adhering to those beneath; and leaves composed of very large leaflets of
an uniform shape and texture. In comparing the three
species with each other, essential differences are observed. The Shellbark Hickory, for instance, and the
Juglans ambigua are constantly distinguished by the number of leaflets, which is always five in the first species, and nine in the last. Their nuts and the entire
fruit, on the other hand, are so much 'alike, that
they might be mistaken for the product of the same
tree; the fruit of both is round with depressed seams,
and the nuts are similarly moulded and equally
white. If, on a more attentive examination, the Glocester Hickory is determined to be a distinct species from
the Thick Shellbark Hickory, it will be observed that
they resemble each other in their leaves, composed
of seven and sometimes of nine leaflets, and in the
luxuriant force of their vegetation; but that they differ
in their fruit, which in the Thick Shellbark Hickory
is oblong with a compressed nut, like that of the
Shellbark Hickory, of twice the size, and of a
yellowish colour, and in the Glocester Hickory
spherical and very large, with a big, greyish white

nut, nearly round, whose shell is two lines thick and extremely hard. In fine, it is to be remarked, that the species and the variety of the Scalybark Hickory which have been described, grow, or at least, are most abundantly multiplied in regions far remote from each other.

PLATE XXXVII.

A leaf of one third of its natural size. Fig. 1, A section of the husk. Fig. 2, Nuts.

PIGNUT HICKORY.

JUGLANS PORCINA. *J. foliolis* 5—7*nis*, *ovato-acuminatis, serratis, glabris : amentis masculis compositis, filiformibus, glabris ; fructu pyriformi vel globoso ; nuce minimâ, levi, durissimâ.*

THIS species is generally known in the United States by the name of Pignut and Hognut Hickory, sometimes also by that of Broom Hickory. The first of these names is most commonly in use; the others are known only in some districts of Pennsylvania and particularly in the County of Lancaster. Portsmouth in New Hampshire may be considered as limiting towards the north, the climate of this tree. A little farther south it is abundant, and in the Atlantic parts of the middle States, it helps, with the Mockernut Hickory, White Oak, Swamp white Oak, Sweet Gum, and Dogwood, to form the mass of the forests. In the Southern States, especially near the coast, it is less common in the woods, being found only on the borders of swamps and in places which are wet without being absolutely marshy, or exposed to be long inundated. This tree is met with in the Western Country, but less frequently, I believe, than the Thick Shellbark and Mockernut Hickories. I have observed that the last mentioned species grows wherever the

Pl. 38

Bosse del.

Gueju se.

Pignut Hickory.

Juglans porcina.

Pignut is found, but that the Pignut does not always accompagny the Mockernut, which is satisfied with a less substantial soil. This remark I have made more particularly in the lower parts of Virginia, of the two Carolinas, and of Georgia. If appears then, that, with the exception of States of Vermont and New Hampshire, of the District of Maine, of the Genesee Country, and of the cold and mountainous tracts along the whole range of the Alleghany mountains, this tree is more or less abundant in the forests, throughout the United States.

The Pignut Hickory is one of the largest trees of the United States. It grows to the height of 70 or 80 feet, with a diameter of 3 or 4 feet. In the winter when stript of its leaves, it is easily known by the shoots of the preceding summer, which are brown, less than half as large as those of the Mockernut and Shellbark Hickories, and terminated by small oval buds. At this season, it is easy also to distinguish the Bitternut Hickory, by its naked and yellow buds. The buds of this species, as in the other Hickories with scaly buds, are more than an inch in length, a few days before their unfolding. The inner scales are the largest and of a reddish colour. The do not fall till the leaves are 5 or 6 inches long. The leaves are compound, and vary in size and in the number of leaflets, according to the moisture and fertility of the soil. In rich grounds, they are 18 inches long; and the complete number of leaflets is 3 pair with an odd one. The leaflets are 4 or 5 inches long, acuminate, serrate, nearly sessile, and glabrous or smooth on both sides. On vigorous trees, which grow in shady exposures, the petiole is of a violet colour.

The barren aments are smooth, filiform, flexible, and pendulous : they are 2 inches long, and in their arrangement, resemble those of the other Hickories. The fertile flowers are greenish, not very conspicuous, and situated at the extremity of the shoot : the fruit succeeds them in pairs as often as single. The husk is thin and of a beautiful green : when ripe, it opens through half its length, for the passage of the nut. The nut is small, smooth, and very hard on account of the thickness of the shell. Its kernel is sweet but meager and difficult to extract, from the firmness of the partitions. These nuts are never carried to market, but serve for food to swine, racoons, and the numerous species of squirrels which people the forests.

In the Pignut Hickory, the form and size of the nuts, vary more than in the other species. Some are oval, and when covered with their husks, resemble young figs ; others are broader than they are long, and others are perfectly round. Among these various forms, some nuts are as large as the thumb, and others not bigger than the little finger. Although the same tree yields fruit of the same form every year, I cannot, after an attentive examination of the young shoots and of the aments, consider these differences in any other light than as va-

· rieties. The two most remarkable of them are described
in the new edition of the *Species plantarum* by Willdenow, as distinct species. That with oblong fruit is called
Juglans glabra, and that with round fruit and a husk
somewhat rough, *Juglans obcordata*. Doctor Muhlen-
berg admits this distinction, but with all the deference
which I owe to his botanical knowledge, I cannot adopt
his opinion.

The wood of the Pignut Hickory resembles that of the
other species, in the colour of its sap and of its heart : it
possesses also their excellencies and their defects. I have
conversed with wheel-wrights in the country, who
affirmed that it is the strongest and the most tenacious
of the Hickories, and who, for that reason, preferred
it to any other for axle-trees and ax-handles. These considerations lead me to recommend its introduction into
the forests of Europe, where its success would be certain.

PLATE XXXVIII.

*A branch with its leaves of one third of the natural
size. Fig.* 1, *A nut with its husk (oblong variety). Fig.* 2, *A
nut without its husk. Fig.* 3, *A nut with its husk (round variety). Fig.* 4, *A nut without its husk.*

NUTMEG HICKORY.

JUGLANS MYRISTICÆFORMIS. *J. foliis quinis, foliolis ovato-acuminatis, serratis, glabris : fructu ovato, scabriusculo ; nuce minimâ, durissimâ.*

No specific denomination has hitherto been given to this species by the inhabitants the Middle States, to which it is peculiar : that of Nutmeg Hickory which I have formed appears sufficiently appropriate, from the resemblance of its nut to a nutmeg.

I have not myself found this tree in the forets, and hence I conclude that it is not common. It is true I had not, at the period of my residence in that part of the United States, conceived the design of the present work, and did not devote myself entirely to the researches, which have since given birth to it. I am acquainted with the Nutmeg Hickory only by a branch and a handfull of nuts, given me at Charleston in the fall of 1802 by the gardener of M'. H. Izard, which he had gathered, in a swamp on his master's plantation of the Elms, in the Parish of Goose creek. From this specimen alone I have included the tree among the Hickories.

The leaves, which are composed of four leaflets with an odd one, are symetrically arranged. I remarked also, that the shoots of the preceding year were flexible and tough.

Nutmeg Hickory Nut .

Juglans myristiceformus .

The nuts are very small, smooth, and of a brown colour marked with lines of white; the husk is thin and somewhat rough on the surface. The shell is so thick that it constitutes two thirds of the volume of the nut, which, consequently, is extremely hard, and has a minute kernel. This fruit is still inferior to the Pignut.

I suspect that the Nutmeg Hickory is more common in Lower Louisiana * : it belongs to inquirers who engage in researches analogous to those which I have pursued in the Atlantic and Western States, to study this tree more fully than I have been able to do, and to complete the imperfect description which I have given of it.

PLATE XXXIX.

A branch and nuts with their husks. Fig. 1, A nut without its husk.

---

* In the interesting work of Mr. W. Darby on Louisiana, published at Philadelphia in 1817, the Nutmeg Hickory is said to abound on the waters of Red river in the Mississipi Territory. *F. A. M.*

RECAPITULATION

OF THE PROPERTIES AND USES

OF HICKORY WOOD.

In the summary introduction to the History of the Walnuts of North America, it was remarked, that those of the second section, or the Hickories, exhibit great variations in the size and shape of their fruit, in the number of leaflets which compose their leaves, and in their general appearance, from the effect of soils of different degrees of moisture. Hence result, in many cases, mutual resemblances so striking, that a person not familiar with this class of trees, might easily confound distinct species, or describe as different species what are mere varieties. On taking of the epidermis or dead part, the same organisation is observed in the bark of all the Hickories. In other trees the fibre and the cellular substance are confounded; here, on the contrary, they are separate, and the fibre is regularly disposed in the form of lozenges, which are smaller in young trees, than in such as are more fully grown. An arrangement so peculiar and remarkable has a beautiful effect, and great advantage might be taken of it in cabinet-making, if this bark was not, like other species, liable to warp. It affords nevertheless an interesting object in vegetable physiology. So close an analogy exists in the wood of these trees, that when stript of the bark, no difference is discernible in the grain, which is coarse and open in all, nor in the colour of the heart, which is uniformly reddish. To these conspicuous properties are added others worthy of remark, which, as has been observed, though modified in the several species, are possessed by them all in a higher degree, than by any other tree of the same latitude in Europe or America. These are great weight, strength, and tenacity, a speedy decay when exposed to heat and moisture, and peculiar liability to injury from worms. According to these prominent excellencies and defects, the uses of their wood are pretty well determined, and to these uses they are indiscriminately applied.

Hickory timber is employed in no part of the United States in the building of houses, because, as has been before observed, it is too heavy, and soon becomes worm eaten. But if its defects forbid its employment in architecture, its good qualities, on the other hand, render it proper for many secondary uses, which could not be as well subserved by any other wood. Throughout the Middle States, it is selected for the axle-trees of carriages, for the handles of axes and other carpenter's tools, and for large screws, particularly those of bookbinder's presses. The cogs of mill-wheels are made of Hickory heart thoroughly seasoned; but it is proper only for such wheels as are not exposed to moisture; and for

this reason some other wood is, by many mill-wrights, preferred. The rods which form the back of Windsor chairs,
coach-whip-handles, musket-stocks, rake-teeth, flails for
threshing grain, the bows of yokes, or the elliptical
pieces which pass under the necks of the cattle; all these
are objects customarily made of Hickory. At Baltimore it is used for the hoops of sieves, and is more esteemed than the White Oak, which is equally elastic, but
more apt to peel off in small shreds into the substance
sifted. In the country near Augusta in Georgia, I have
remarked that the common chairs are of Hickory wood.
In New Jersey it is employed for shoeing sledges, that is,
for covering the runners or parts which slide upon the
snow; but to be proper for this use it must have been
cut long enough to have become perfectly dry.

Of the numerous trees of North America east. of the
Alleghany mountains, none except the Hickory is perfectly adapted to the making of hoops for casks and
boxes. For this purpose vast quantities of it are consumed at home, and exported to the West India Islands.
The hoops are made of young Hickories from 6 to 12 feet
high, without choice as to the species. The largest hoop-
poles sold at Philadelphia and New York in February
1808, at three dollars a hundred. Each pole is split into
two parts, and the hoop is crossed and confined by
notches, instead of being bound at the end with twigs,
like those made of Chesnut. From the solidity of the
wood, this method appears sufficiently secure.

When it is considered how large a part of the productions of the United States is packed for exportation
in barrels, an estimate may be formed of the necessary
consumption of hoops. In consequence of it, young
trees proper for this object have become scarce in all
parts of the country which have long been settled. The
evil is greater, as they do not sprout a second time
from the ame root, and as their growth is slow.
The cooper can not lay up a store of them for future
use, for unless employed within a year, and often
within six months after being cut, they are attacked by
two species of insect; one of these, which eats within
the wood, and commits the greatest ravages, is represented on the plate of the Mockernut Hickory, the wood of
which species I have observed to be peculiarly liable to
its attacks.

The defects which unfit the Hickory for use in
the building of houses, equally exclude it from the
construction of vessels. At New York and Philadelphia,
the Shellbark and Pignut Hickories have been taken for
keels, and are found to last as long as those of other
wood, owing to their being always in the water. Of
the two species, the Pignut would be preferable as being
less liable to split, but it is rarely found of as large dimensions as the other.

In sloops and schooners the rings by which the sails
are hoisted and confined to the mast, are always of
Hickory. I have also been assured, that for attaching the

cordage it makes excellent pegs, which are stronger than those of Oak: but they should set loosely in the holes, as otherwise for want of speedily seasoning, they soon decay. For handspikes the Hickory is particulary esteemed on account of its strength : it is accordingly employed in most American vessels, and is exported for the same purpose to England, where it sells from 5o to ⏀o per cent higher than Ash, which is brought also from the North of the United States. The Hickories are cut without distinction for this use, but the Pignut, I believe, is the best.

All the Hickories are very heavy, and in a given volume contain a great quantity of combustible matter. They produce an ardent heat, and leave a heavy, compact, and long lived coal. In this respect, no wood of the same latitude, in Europe or America, can be compared to them : such, at least, is the opinion of all Europeans who have resided in the United States. At New York, Philadelphia and Baltimore, people in easy circumstances, burn no other wood, and though it is sold 5o per cent higher than Oak, it is found profitable iu use. It sold at New York the 20th of october 1807 at 15 dollars a cord, and Oak wood at 10 dollars. From its superior quality, the Hickory is always sold separately. I have noticed that at New York, the Shellbark predominated in the fuel, and at Philadelphia and Baltimore, the Mockernut. At Baltimore the Shellbark, easily recognised by its scaly bark, is never seen.

The quantity of the respective species of Hickory consumed in the cities, is regulated by a soil and climate, more favorable to one than another, and not by an opinion entertained of their comparative excellence; though experience shews the Mockernut to be the best and the Bitternut the poorest. This difference, however, is too slight to be generally regarded.

Of the uses to which the Hickory is devoted in the United States, two will principally contribute, together with the slowness of its growth, to its entire extermination; these are, the cutting of the saplings for hoops, and of the trees for fuel. These considerations independantly of many accessory causes, which hasten the destruction of the forests in this part of the new world, lead me to believe, that in lest than 5o years, they will not furnish a tenth part of the hoops demanded in commerce. Hence arise motives sufficiently powerful to engage proprietors, who seek to preserve their woods, and to augment their value, to multiply in them the most useful trees, and especially the Hickories. The object might be fully attained by planting walnuts, previously made to germinate in boxes filled with earth, and kept moist in the cellar: the success of this simple method is certain. It would be advantageous also, to plant a greater number than the soil can sustain, that when the poles are an inch in diameter, a part of them may be cut for hoops, while the rest are left to grow for fuel, or for other uses to which the Hickory is appropriate.

It has been seen by what precedes, that though the Hickory wood has essential defects, they are compensated by good properties which render it valuable in the arts, and which entitle it to the attention of Europeans ; above all, as a combustible. Though its growth is slow during its early years, it should form a part of our forests. But I doubt whether this can be effected except by planting nuts in the woods, for the trees, even when very young, with difficulty survive transplantation. Before they are 3 lines in diameter and 18 inches tall, they have a tap root 3 feet long and destitute of fibres. Hence it has happened, that of more than a hundred thousand young plants, produced by nuts which I have at different times sent to France, very few are found alive. They have perished in the removal from the nursery, or in the second transplantation to the place of their ultimate destination. The Black Walnut and Bitternut, on the contrary, whose roots do not descend deeply and are plentifully garnished with fibres, easily recover themselves after transplantation, even when 6 or 8 feet high at the time of their removal.

In concluding this article I recommend particulary for propagation in European forests the Shellbark Hickory and the Pignut Hickory, whose wood unites in the highest degree the valuable properties of the group. I think also that the Pacanenut merits attention from promoters of useful culture, not so much for its wood as for its fruit, which is excellent and more deli-

cate than that of the European Walnut. It might probably be doubled in size, if the practice was successfully
adopted of grafting this species upon the Black Walnut
or upon the Common European Walnut.

———

MAPLES.

Of the species which compose this genus, the number known is already considerable, and will probably be augmented by the future researches of Botanists, especially on the continent of North America.

The Maples, in general, are lofty and beautiful trees. One of their principal characters consists in opposite leaves divided into several very distinct lobes. Capable of enduring an intense degree of cold, they form in the North of the Old and of the New continent, extensive forests, which, with those of the Beech, appear to succeed the Spruce, the Larch, and the Pine, and to precede the Chesnut and the Oak. Such, at least, seems to be in America between the 43 and 46 degrees of latitude, the place assigned by nature to the true Sugar Maple.

The species of Maples hitherto described amount to fourteen, of which seven belong to Europe, and seven to North America. Among these last I have not included the Dwarf Red Maple, *Acer coccineum*, which is a diminutive species, and concerning which I do not possess adequate materials for a description. It abounds in Nova Scotia and has always been confounded with the proper Red Maple; I have also observed it in the upper parts of New Hampshire. It scarcely exceeds 12 or 18 feet in height, and its flowers and seeds are of a more vivid red than those of the Red Maple. The Black sugar Maple

I.   27

grows to about the same height with the Sugar Maple, but it is plainly a distinct species. In the collection of dried plants made by Cap ᵘ. Lewis and Clarke during their journey to the south sea, I saw specimens of a beautiful Maple from the banks of Columbia river.

From this brief summary it results that the North American species are more numerous than those of Europe. The wood of the Maples differs so widely in quality in different species, that it becomes difficult to characterize it by general observations: it may be remarked that it speedily ferments and decays when exposed to the weather, that it is liable to be injured by worms, and that hence, it is unfit for building. It possesses properties however, which compensate in part for these defects, and which render it useful in the arts and in domestic economy. For more particular information, I must refer the reader to the descriptions of the respective species.

METHODICAL DISPOSITION

OF THE MAPLES

OF NORTH AMERICA,

INCLUDING TWO EUROPEAN SPECIES.

———

Polygamia dioecia, LINN. *Acera*, JUSS.

1.st SECTION.

Sessile flowers. Fructification vernal.

1. White Maple. . . . . . . *Acer eriocarpum.*
2. Red flowering Maple. . . *Acer rubrum.*

2.d SECTION.

Pedunculated flowers. Fructification autumnal.

3. Sugar Maple . . . . *Acer saccharinum.*
4. Black sugar Maple. . . . . *Acer nigrum.*
5. Norway Maple. . . . . . . *Acer platanoides.*
6. Sycamore. . . . . *Acer pseudo-platanus.*
7. Moose wood. . . . . *Acer striatum.*
8. Box elder. . . . . *Acer negundo.*
9. Mountain Maple. . . . . . *Acer montanum.*

Bessa del.

Gabriel sc

White Maple.
Acer eriocárpum.

WHITE MAPLE.

Acer eriocarpum. A. foliis oppositis, quinquelobis, pro-
fundè sinuatis, inæqualiter dentatis, subtùs candidissi-
mis : floribus pentandris, apetalis.

In the Atlantic parts of the United States, this species
is often confounded with the Red Maple which it nearly
resembles; west of the Mountains, they are constantly
distinguished, and the *Acer eriocarpum* is known by no
other name than White Maple.

The banks of Sandy river in the District of Maine, and
those of the Connecticut near Windsor in Vermont, are
the most northern points at which I have seen the White
Maple. But, like many other vegetables, it is pinched by
the rigorous winters of this latitude, and never reaches
the size which it attains a few degrees farther south.
It is found on the banks of all the rivers which flow from
the mountains to the Ocean, though it is less common
along the streams which water the southern parts
of the Carolinas and of Georgia. In no part of the
United States is it more multiplied than in the western
country, and nowhere is its vegetation more luxuriant than
on the banks of the Ohio, and of the great rivers which
empty into it. There, sometimes alone, and sometimes
mingled with the Willow, which is found along all these
waters, it contributes singularly by its magnificent fo-

liage to the embellishment of the scene. The brilliant white of the leaves beneath forms a striking contrast with the bright green above, and the alternate reflexion of the two surfaces in the water, heightens the beauty of this wonderful moving mirror, and aids in forming an enchanting picture, which, during my long excursions in a canoe in these regions of solitude and silence, I contemplated with unwearied admiration. Beginning at Pittsburgh, and even some miles above the junction of the Alleghany and Monongahela rivers, White Maples 12 or 15 feet in circumference are continually met with at short distances.

The trunk of this tree is low, and divides itself into a greatn umber of limbs so divergent, that they form a head more spacious than that of any other tree with which I am acquainted. It is worthy of remark, that the White Maple is found on the banks of such rivers only as have limpid waters and a gravelly bed, and never in swamps and other wet grounds inclosed in forests, where the soil is black and miry. These situations, on the contrary, are so well adapted to the Red Maple, that they are frequently occupied by it exclusively. Hence the last mentioned species is common in the Lower parts of the Carolinas and of Georgia, where the White Maple is no longer seen; for as soon as the rivers, in descending from the mountains towards the Ocean, reach the low country, they begin to be bordered by miry swamps covered with the Cypress, Blackgum, Large Tupelo, etc.

The White Maple blooms early in the spring : its flowers are small and sessile with a downy *ovarium*. The fruit is larger than that of any other species which grows east of the Mississipi. It consists of two capsules joined at the base, each of which encloses one roundish seed, and is terminated by a large, membraneous, falciform wing. In Pennsylvania it is ripe about the 1st. of May and a month earlier on the Savannah river, in Georgia. At this period, the leaves which have attained half their size are very downy underneath ; a month later, when fully grown, they are perfectly smooth. They are opposite and supported by long petioles ; they are divided by deep sinuses into four lobes, are toothed on the edges, of a bright green on the upper surface, and of a beautiful white beneath. The foliage however is scattered and leaves an open thoroughfare to the sun beams.

The wood of this Maple is very white, and of a fine grain ; but it is softer and lighter than that of the other species in the United States, and from its want of strength and durability it is little used. Wooden bowls are sometimes made of it when Poplar cannot be procured. At Pittsburgh, and in the neighbouring towns, it serves in cabinet-making, instead of Holly, for inlaying furniture of Mahogany, Cherry tree, and Walnut: though it is less proper for this purpose, as it soon changes colour. The hatters of Pittsburgh prefer the charcoal of this wood to every other for heating their boilers, as it affords a heat more uniform, and

of longer continuance. Some of the inhabitants on
the Ohio make sugar of its sap, by the same process
which is employed with the Sugar Maple. Like the Red
Maple, it yields but half the product from a given measure
of sap ; but the unrefined sugar is whiter and more
agreeable to the taste than that of the Sugar Maple.
The sap is in motion earlier in this species than in the
Sugar Maple, beginning to ascend about the 15th of
January ; so that the work of extracting the sugar is
sooner completed. The cellular integument rapidly
produces a black precipitate with sulphate of iron.

In all parts of the United States where this tree
abounds, many others are found of superior value :
its secondary consequence is evinced by the unimportant uses to which it is devoted.

In Europe, the White Maple is multiplied in nurseries and gardens. Its rapid growth affords hopes of
cultivating it with profit in this quarter of the world,
which is less rich in the diversity of its species. In forming plantations, more care than has hitherto been
taken, should be paid to the choice of the ground, which
should be constantly moist, or exposed to annual inundations : in such situations its vegetation would be supri-
singly beautiful and rapid.

PLATE XL.

*A branch, with leaves of the natural size. Fig. 1, Barren
flowers. Fig. 2, Fertile flowers. Fig. 3, A seed of the natural
size.*

Red flowering Maple.

Acer rubrum.

Pl. 4.

RED FLOWERING MAPLE.

Acer rubrum. *A. foliis oppositis, trilobis, inæqualiter dentatis, subtus glaucis : floribus rubris, aggregatis ; germine glaberrimo ; umbellis sessilibus : capsulis rubris, pedunculatis.*

Different names are given to this tree in different parts of the United States : east of the Alleghany mountains it is called Red flowering Maple, Swamp Maple and Soft Maple; in the Western Country, simply Maple. The first denomination, which is most generally in use, is also most appropriate, as the young shoots, the flowers, and the fruit are red.

. Toward the north, the Red flowering Maple, appears first about Malebaye, in Canada, in the latitude of 48°; but it soon become more common in proceeding southward, and is found abundant to the extremities of Florida and Lower Louisiana. Of all the trees which flourish in wet grounds occasionnally overflowed, this species is most multiplied in the Middle and Southern States. It occupies, in great part, the borders of the creeks, and abounds in all the swamps which are often inun--dated, and always miry. In these situations, it is accompanied by the Blackgum, Sweetgum, Shellbark Hickory, Swamp White Oak, Black Ash and White Ash. To these are added in the Carolinas and Georgia, the Small Magnolia or Swamp Bay, the Water Oak, Loblolly Bay, Tupelo, and Red Bay. It is a remarkable fact, that west of the mountains, between Brownsville and Pittsburgh, the Red flowering Maple is seen growing on elevated ground with the Oaks and the Walnuts. I have nowhere observed it of as ample dimensions as in Pennsylvania and New Jersey : in these States exist extensive marshes, called Maple swamps, exclusively covered with it, where it is found 70 feet high and 3 or 4 feet in diameter.

The Red flowering Maple is the earliest tree whose bloom announces the return of spring; it is in flower near New York from the 10 to the 15 of April. The blossoms of a beautiful purple or deep red, unfold more than a fornight before the leaves. They are sessile, aggregate, and situated at the extremity of the branches. The fruit is suspended by long flexible peduncles and is of the same hue; with the flowers, though it varies in size and in the intensity of its colouring, according to the exposure and dampness of the soil. The leaves are smaller than those of the preceding species, but in some respects, they resemble them. They are glaucous or whitish underneath, and are palmated or divided into 3 or 4 acuminate lobes, irregularly toothed. The extremities of this tree, which are formed by numerous twigs united at the base, have a remarkable appearance when garnished with flowers and seeds of a deep red, before vegetation has begun generally to revive.

Before the Red flowering Maple exceeds 25 or 30.

feet in height and 7 or 8 inches in diameter, its bark is perfectly smooth, and marked with white blotches, by which it is easily distinguishable. Afterwards, the trunk, like that of the White Oak and Sweet Gum, becomes brown and chapped. In this tree, as in others which grow in wet places, the sap bears a large proportion to the heart, if indeed the name of heart can properly be given to the irregular star which occupies the center of large trunks, with points, from 1 to 5 inches in length., projecting into the sap.

The wood of the Red flowering Maple is applicable to interesting uses. It is harder than that of the White Maple, and of a finer and closer grain : hence it is easily wrought in the lathe., and acquires by polishing a glossy and silken surface. It is sufficiently solid, and for many purposes it is preferred by workmen to other kinds of wood. It is principally employed for the lower part of Windsor chairs : the pieces are turned in the country, and so considerable is the demand, that boats laden with them arrive at New York and Philadelphia, where an extensive manufacture is carried on, for the consumption of the neighbouring towns, and for exportation to the Southern States and to the West India Islands. The whole frame of japanned chairs is of this wood, except the back, for which Hickory is chosen on account of its superior strength and elasticity. The frame, the nave, and the spokes of spinning wheels are made of it : at Philadelphia it is exclusively employed for saddle trees , and in the country it is preferred for yokes , and also for shovels and wooden dishes', which are brought to market , and purchased by the dealers in wooden ware.

It sometimes happens that in very old trees, the grain instead of following a perpendicular direction, is undulated, and this variety bears the name of Curled Maple. This singular arrangement , of which I am able to assign no cause , is never witnessed in young trees , nor in the branches of such as exhibit it in the trunk : it is also less conspicious at the center , than near the circumference. Trees offering this disposition are rare , and do not exist in the proportion of one to a hundred. The serpentine direction of the fibre , which renders them difficult to split and to work , produces in the hands of a skilful mechanic , the most beautiful effects of light and shade. These effects are rendered more striking, if , after smoothing the surface of the wood with a double ironed plane , it is rubbed with a little sulphuric acid , and afterwards anointed with linseed oil. On examining it attentively, the varying shades are found to be owing entirely to the inflexion of the rays of light ; which is more sensibly perceived in viewing it in different directions by candle light.

Before Mahogany became generally fashionable in the United States , the most beautiful furniture was of Red flowering Maple , and bedsteads are still made of it , which, in richness and lustre, exceed the finest Mahogany.

At Boston some cabinet-makers saw it into thin
plates for inlaying Mahogany. But the most constant
use of the Curled Maple is for the stocks of fowling
pieces and rifles, which to elegance and lightness unite
a solidity resulting from the accidental direction of the
fibre.

The cellular integument of the Red flowering Maple
is of a dusky red. By boiling, it yields a purplish colour,
which, on the addition of sulphate of iron, becomes dark
blue approaching to black. It is used in the country,
with a certain portion of Alum in solution, for dying
black.

The wood of the Red flowering Maple does not burn
well, and is so little esteemed for fuel that it is rarely
brought into the cities.

The French Canadians make sugar from the sap of
this Maple, which they call *Plaine*, but, as in the preceding species, the product of a given measure is only half
as great as is obtained from the Sugar Maple.

It should be observed that the Red flowering Maple
never attains its full dimensions except in swamps where
the bottom is composed of fertile soil. When the population of the country becomes denser, these tracts will be
cleared and improved by some mode of culture more.
profitable than the growth of woods, and especially
of this species, which is fit neither for the uses of the
wheelwright nor for any other solid work; for it
possesses little strength, is liable to injury from worms,

and ferments and speedily decays when exposed to the
alternations of dryness and moisture. Though at present
it is extensively used, its importance in the arts it not such
as to entitle it to preservation, and it will doubtless one day
become rare. When the period arrives that it is necessary
in the United States, as in Europe, to renew the forests,
or to keep on foot those which have escaped destruction,
the American Woodman will find among the Oaks, the
Walnuts, and the Ashes, many species more deserving of
his care. The Sugar Maple also will be preferred, which
grows on uplands, and possesses in a superior degree
all the good properties of the other. From these considerations the Red flowering Maple appears to have no pretensions to a place in European forests.

PLATE XLI.

*A branch with leaves of the natural size. Fig. 1, Barren
flowers. Fig. 2, Fertile flowers. Fig. 3, Seeds of the natural
size.*

Pl. 42

Sugar Maple.

Acer saccharinum.

SUGAR MAPLE.

ACER SACCHARINUM. A. *foliis quinque-partito-palmatis,
glabris, margine integris, subtus glaucis : floribus pedunculatis, pendentibus.*

THIS species, the most interesting of the American
Maples, is called Rock Maple, Hard Maple, and Sugar
Maple. The first of these names is most generaly in use,
but I have preserved the last, because it indicates one
of the most valuable properties of the tree.

According to my father's researches into the topography
of American vegetables, the Sugar Maple begins a little
north of Lake St. John, in Canada, near the 48° of latitude, which, in the rigour of its winter, corresponds
to the 68° in Europe. It is nowhere more abundant
than between the 46° and 43°, which comprise Canada,
New Brunswick, Nova Scotia, the States of Vermont
and New Hampshire, and the District of Maine : in these
regions, it enters largely into the composition of the
forests with which they are still covered. Farther south,
it is common only in Genessee in the State of New
York, and in the Upper parts of Pennsylvania. It is
estimated by Dʳ Rush, that in the northern parts of
these two States, there are ten millions of acres which
produce these trees in the proportion of 3o to an acre.
Indeed I have noticed, in traversing these districts,
large masses of woods formed of them almost exclusively.

In Genessee, however, a great part of the Maples belong to a species which I shall describe, which has hitherto been confounded by Botanists with the Sugar Maple.

In the lowers parts of Virginia, of the Carolinas, and of 'Georgia, and likewise in the Mississipi Territory, this tree is unknown or very rare. It is rapidly disappearing from the forests about New York and Philadelphia, where it is no longer drained for sugar, but is felled for fuel and for other purposes.

Between the parallels mentioned as bounding the tracts where this tree is most abundant, the forests do not resemble those of a more southern latitude : they are composed of two different descriptions of trees divided into two great classes, which alternately occupy the soil and which exist in nearly equal proportions. The first class comprises the resinous trees such as Pines and Spruces, and covers the low grounds and the bottoms of the vallies; these forests are called *Black wood lands*. The second class consist of leafy trees, such as the Sugar Maple, the White and the Red Beech, the Birches and the Ashes; of which the Sugar Maple is most multiplied. They grow on level grounds or on gentle declivities, and form what are denominated *Hard wood lands*. In proceeding from the 46° of latitude northward, the trees of the second class are observed to become more rare, and the resinous trees in the same proportion more abundant : below 43°, on the other hand, the resinous trees are found less common, and the others loose their predominance in the forests, as they become mingled with the numerous species of Oaks and Walnuts.

The Sugar Maple covers a greater extent of the American soil than any other species of this genus. It flourishes most in mountainous places, where the soil though fertile is cold and humid. Besides the parts which I have particularly mentioned, where the face of the country is generally of this nature, it is found along the whole chain of the Alleghanies to their termination in Georgia, and on the steep and shady banks of the rivers which rise in these mountains.

The Sugar Maple reaches the height of 70 or 80 feet with a proportional diameter; but it does not commonly exceed 50 or 60 feet with a diameter of 12 or 18 inches. Well grown, thriving trees are beautiful in their appearance, and easily distinguishable by the whiteness of their bark. The leaves are about 5 inches broad, but they vary in length according to the age and vigour of the tree. They are opposite, attached by long petioles, palmated or unequally divided into five lobes, entire at the edges, of a bright green above, and glaucous or whitish underneath. In autumn, they turn reddish with the first frosts. Except in the colour of the lower surface they nearly resemble the leaves of the Norway Maple. The flowers are small, yellowish, and suspended by slender, drooping peduncles. The seed is contained in two capsules united at base and terminated in a membraneous wing. It is ripe near New York in the beginning of October, though the capsules attain their full size six weeks earlier. Externally they appear equally perfect, but I have constantly found one of them empty. The fruit is matured only once in two or three years.

The wood when cut is white, but after being wrought and exposed for some time to the light, it takes a rosy tinge. Its grain is fine and close, and when polished, it has a silky lustre. It is very strong and sufficiently heavy, but wants the property of durability, for which the Chesnut and the Oak are so highly esteemed. When exposed to moisture it soon decays, and for this reason it is neglected in civil and naval architecture. In Vermont, New Hampshire, the District of Maine and farther north, where the Oak is not plentiful, this timber is substituted for it, in preference to the Beech, the Birch, and the Elm. When perfectly seasoned, which requires two or three years, it is used by Wheelwrights for axle-trees and spokes, and for lining the runners of common sleds. It is also employed as well as the Red flowering Maple in the manufacture of Windsor chairs. In the country where the houses are wholly of wood, Sugar Maple timber is admitted into the frame; and in the District of Maine, it is preferred to the Beech for the keels of vessels, as it furnishes longer pieces: with the Beech and the Yellow Pine it forms also the lower frame, which is always in the water.

This wood exhibits two accidental forms in the arrangement of the fibre, of which cabinet-makers take advantage for making beautiful articles of furniture. The first consists in undulations like those of the Curled Maple, the second, which take places only in old trees that are still sound, and which appears to arise from an inflexion of the fibre from the circumference toward the center, produces spots of half a line in diameter, sometimes contiguous, and sometimes several lines apart. The more numerous the spots, the more beautiful and the more esteemed is the wood : this variety is called Bird's eye Maple. Like the Curled Maple it is used for inlaying Mahogany, Bedsteads are made of it and portable writing desks, which are elegant and highly prized. To obtain the finest effect, the log should be sawn in a direction as nearly as possible parallell to the concentrical circles.

When cut at the proper season the Sugar Maple forms excellent fuel. It is exported from District of Maine for the consumption of Boston, and is equally esteemed with the Hickory. The opinion entertained of it in this respect, in the North of America, accords with the interesting experiments of M' Hartig on the comparative heat afforded by different species of European wood, from which it results, that the Sycamore, *Acer pseudo-platanus*, is superior to every other.

The ashes of the Sugar Maple are rich in the alkaline principle, and it may be confidently asserted, that theyfurnish four fifths of the potash exported to Europe from Boston and New York.

In the forges of Vermont and the District of Maine, the charcoal of this wood is preferred to any other, and it is said to be one fifth heavier than the coal made from the same species in the Middle and Southern States ; a fact which sufficiently evinces that this Maple acquires its characteristic properties in perfection, only in' nor-thern climates.

The wood of the Sugar Maple is easily distinguished from that of the Red flowering Maple, which it resembles in appearance, by its weight and hardness. There is, besides, a very simple and certain test : a few drops of sulphate of iron being poured on samples of the different species, the Sugar Maple turns greenish, and the White Maple and Red flowering Maple change to a deep blue.

The extraction of sugar from the Maple is a valuable resource in a country, where all classes of society daily make use of tea and coffee.

The process by which it is obtained is very simple, and is every where nearly the same. Though not essentially defective, it might be rendered more perfect and more profitable, by adopting hints which have been thrown out in American publications.

The work is commonly taken in hand in the month of February, or in the beginning of March, while the cold continues intense, and the ground is still covered with snow. The sap begins to be in motion at this season, two months before the general revival of vegetation. In a central situation, lying convenient to the trees from which the sap is drawn, a shed is constructed, called a sugar camp, which is destined to shelter the boilers and the persons who tend them, from the weather. An auger 3/4 of an inch in diameter, small troughs to receive the sap, tubes of Elder or Sumac, 8 or 10 inches long, corresponding in size to the auger, and laid open for a part of their length, buckets for emptying the troughs and conveying the sap to the camp, boilers of 15 or 18 gallons' capacity, moulds to receive the sirop when reduced to a proper consistency for being formed into cakes, and lastly, axes to cut and split the fuel, are the principal ustensils employed in the operation.

The trees are perforated in an obliquely ascending direction, 18 or 20 inches from the ground, with two holes 4 or 5 inches apart. Care should be taken that the augers do not enter more than half an inch within the wood, as experience has shewn the most abundant flow of sap to take place at this depth. It is also recommended to insert the tubes on the south side of the tree; but this useful hint is not always attended to.

The troughs, which contain 2 or 3 gallons, are made in the Northern States, of White Pine, of White or Black Oak, or of Maple; on the Ohio, the Mulberry, which is very abundant, is preferred. The Chesnut, the Black

Walnut , and the Butternut should be rejected , as they impart to the liquid the colouring matter and bitter principle , with which they are impregnated.

A trough is placed on the ground at the foot of each tree , and the sap is every day collected and temporarily poured into casks, from which it is drawn out to fill the boilers. The evaporation is kept up by a brisk fire , and the skum is carefully taken off during this part of the process. Fresh sap is added from time to time , and the heat is maintained till the liquid is reduced to a sirop , after which it is left to cool, and then strained through a blanket or other woolen stuff, to separate the remain-ing impurities.

Some persons recommend leaving the sirop twelve hours , before boiling it for the last time ; others pro-ceed with it immediately. In either case , the boilers are only half filled , and by an active, steady heat, the li-quor is rapidly reduced to the proper consistency for being poured into the moulds. The evaporaration is known to have proceeded far enough , when , upon rub-bing a drop of the sirop between the fingers , it is per-ceived to be granular. If it is in danger of boiling over , a bit of lard or of butter, is thrown into it, which in-stantly calms the ebullition. The molasses being drained off from the moulds, the sugar is no longer deliquescent , like the raw sugar of the West Indies.

Maple Sugar manufactured in this way , is lighter col-oured , in proportion to the care with which it is made and the judgment with which the evaporation is conducted. It is superior to the brown Sugar of the Colonies, at least, to such as is generally used in the United States : its taste is as pleasant, and it is as good for culinary purposes. When refined, it equals in beauty the finest Sugar consumed in Europe. It is made use of, however, only in the districts where it is made, and there, only in the country : from prejudice or taste, imported sugar is used in all the small towns, and in the inns.

The sap continues to flow for six weeks ; after which, it becomes less abundant, less rich in saccharine matter, and sommetimes even incapable of chrystalisation. In this case, it is consumed in the state of molasses, which is superior to that of the Islands. After three or four days exposure to the sun, Maple sap is converted into vinegar, by the acetous fermention.

In a periodical work, published at Philadelphia several years since, the following receipt is given for making Sugar Maple beer : Upon 4 gallons of boiling water, pour 1 quart of Maple molasses; add a little yeast or leaven to excite the fermentation, and a spoonful of the essence of spruce : a very pleasant and salutary drink is thus obtained.

The process for extracting the sugar which I have described is the most common one, and it is the same from whatever species of Maple the sugar is made.

The amount of sugar manufactured in a year varies from different causes. A cold and dry winter renders the

trees more productive than a changeable and humid
season. It is observed, that when a frosty night is followed by a dry and brilliant day, the sap flows abundantly; and 2 or 3 gallons are sometimes yielded by a
single tree, in twenty four hours. Three persons are
found sufficient to tend 250 trees, which give 1000
pounds of sugar, or 4 pounds from each tree. But this
product is not uniform, for many farmers on the Ohio
have assured me, that they did not commonly obtain
more than 2 pounds from a tree.

Trees which grow in low and moist places afford a
greater quantity of sap than those which occupy rising
grounds, but it is less rich in the saccharine principle.
That of insulated trees, left standing in the middle of
fields or by the side of fences, is the best. It is also
remarked, that in districts which have been cleared of
other trees, and even of the less vigorous Sugar Maples, the product of the remainder is, proportionally,
most considerable.

While I resided in Pittsburgh, the following curious
particulars appeared in the Greensburgh Gazette : « Having introduced » says the writer, « twenty tubes into a
Sugar Maple, I drew from it the same day, 23 gallons
and 3 quarts of sap, which gave 7 pounds and a quarter
of sugar : 33 pounds have been made this season from the
same tree ; which supposes 100 gallons of sap. » It appears here, that only a little more than 3 gallons, was
required for a pound, though four are commonly allowed.

In the foregoing experiments, 5 quarts were drawn in one day from each tube, which is about equal to to the quantity discharged, when two pipes are employed. Might it not hence be concluded, that the sap escapes only from the orifices of the vessels, which have been divided by the auger, without being diverted to this issue, from the neighbouring parts? I am the more inclined to this opinion, as in rambling one day, in the profound solitude of the forests, on the banks of the Ohio, the idea suggested itself to me of cutting into a Maple which had been bored the preceding year. I found amid the white mass of its wood, a green column, equal in width and in depth to the hole beneath. The organisation appeared not to be affected; but this is not sufficient to warrant the conclusion, that these vessels would be in condition to give passage to the sap, the succeeding year. It may be objected, that trees have been drained for 5o years, without diminution of their produce. But a tree of two or three feet in diameter, presents an extensive surface, and the tubes are every year shifted : besides, the successive layers of 3o or 4o years, would restore it nearly to the state of one that never had been perforated.

In the United States, Maple sugar is made in greatest quantities, it the upper part of New Hampshire, in Vermont, in the State of New York, particularly in Genesee, and in the Counties of Pennsylvania which

lie on the eastern and western branches of the Susquehannah ; west of the mountains , in the country borde-
ring on the Alleghany , Mononghahela , and Ohio rivers.
The farmers , after laying aside a sufficient store for
their own consumption , sell the residue to the shop-
keepers in the small towns of the neighbourhood , at
8 cents a pound , by whom it is retailed at 11 cents. A
great deal of sugar is also made , in Upper Canada , and
on the Wabash near Michillimackinac. The Indians dis-
pose of it to the commissioners of the North Western
Company established at Montreal , for the use of the
numerous agents who go out in their employ , in
quest of furs , beyond Lake Superior. In Nova Scotia and
the District of Maine , and on the highest mountains
of Virginia and the Carolinas , where these trees are
sufficiently common , the manufacture is less considerable , and probably six sevenths of the inhabitants
consume imported sugar.

It has been advanced , and doubtless correctly , that
the northern parts of New York and Pennsylvania contain Maples enough to supply the whole consumption
of the United States. But the annual produce by no means
answers to this patriotic calculation. The trees grow

---

* The annual consumption of sugar in the United States is about
80 millions of pounds ; of which more than 50 millions of pounds
are imported ; more than 10 millions produced by the cane in Louisiana ; and, probably, as much as 10 millions made from the Sugar
Maple.

upon excellent lands, which by the influx of emigrants
from the older settlements, and by the surprising increase
of the population already established, are rapidly clear-
-ing ; so that in less, perhaps, than half a century, the
Maples will be confined to exposures too steep for cultivation, and will afford no resource, except to the
proprietor on whose domain they grow. At this period
also, the wood will probably produce a greater and more
ready profit than the sugar. It has been proposed to plant
Sugar Maples in orchards or about the fields : but
would it not be more certainly advantageous to multiply
the Apple tree, which grows in soils too dry to sustain the
vegetation of the Maple? All that has been said on this
subject , must be considered as speculative merely ,
since , in the Eastern States , where information is generally diffused , no enterprises of this nature have been
undertaken, by which the importation of sugar might
be diminished.

Wild and domestic animals are inordinately fond of
Maple juice, and break through their enclosures to sate
themselves with it.

The details into which I have entered, concerning the
Sugar Maple, furnish the means of estimating its importance, with reference both to its sap, and to its
wood. I have indicated the regions where it grows,
and the soil in which it thrives; and I feel authorised
in seriously recommending it for propagation in the
North of Europe. Its sap and its wood are superior to

those of the Norway Maple and of the Sycamore, and in the same countries where these two species abound in the forests, its success would be most complete, and its cultivation most profitable.

PLATE XLIL

A branch with leaves and seeds of the natural size. Fig. 1, A small twig with flowers.

Pl. 4.

Black Sugar Maple.
Acer nigrum.

BLACK SUGAR TREE.

ACER NIGRUM. A. *foliis quinque-partito-palmatis, sinubus apertis, margine integra, subtùs pubescentibus, atro-viridibus : floribus corymbis : capsulis turgidè subglobosis.*

IN the Western States, and in the parts of Pennsylvania and Virginia, which lie between the mountains and the Ohio, this species of Maple is designated by the name of Sugar Tree, and frequently, by the more characteristic denomination of Black Sugar Tree ; probably, on account of the dark colour of its leaves, in comparison with those of the true Sugar Maple, which sometimes grows with it. In the extensive country of Genesee both species are indiscriminately called Rock Maple and Sugar Maple. This confusion seems to have arisen from the country's being settled principally by emigrants from the Eastern States, who, finding the Black Sugar Tree applicable to the same uses with the other, and equally productive of sugar, have given it the same name. The two species have also been confounded by Botanists, in describing the vegetable productions of America.

Towards the north, I first observed the Black Sugar Tree, near Windsor in Vermont, on the Connecticut river. But from its inferior size, and its scarceness, it

may be inferred that it belongs to a more southern
climate. Accordingly , a few degrees lower , it forms a
large part of the forests of Genesee , and covers the
immense vallies , through which flow the great rivers
of the West. In these bottoms* it is one of the most common and one of the loftiest trees.

The leaves are 4 or 5 inches long , and exibit , in every
respect , nearly the same conformation as those of the
true Sugar Maple. They differ from them , principally ,
in being of a deeper green and of a thicker texture, and
in having more open sinuses : they are also slightly
downy , which is most sensibly perceptible on the main
rib.

The flowers , like those of the Sugar Maple , are suspended by long , flexible peduncles : the seeds , also ,
are similar , and are ripe about the same time , that is ,
about the 1ˢᵗ of October.

The wood is much like that of the other species, but
it is coarser-grained , and less brilliant when polished.
It is little used , because , wherever it abounds , other
trees are found , such as the Oak , the Walnut , the
Cherry tree , and the Mulberry , which are more esteemed for building and for cabinet making. It is, however , preferred for the frames of Windsor chairs , and
is considered after the Hickories as the best fuel. Its

---

* This word has become authorised by general use in the United
States.

most important use is for making Sugar, of which it
annually yields a vast amount, in the neighbourhood
of Pittsburgh.

When the Black Sugar Tree stands alone, it naturally
assumes a regular and agreeable shape. Its foliage, of a
darker tint and more tufted than that of the other Maples, renders it proper for forming avenues, and for
adorning parks and gardens; in fine, for every situation
where thick shade is desired, as a shelter from the sun.

PLATE XLIII.

A branch with a leaf and seeds of the natural size.

NORWAY MAPLE.

ACER PLATANOIDES. A. *foliis quinque-lobis, acuminatis, utrinque glabris, lobis dentatis : corymbosis erectis, pedunculis glabris.*

THIS species of Maple is found in the same parts of Europe with the Sycamore, but it is most multiplied in Sweden and Norway; whence it has received the name of Norway Maple.

Like the Sycamore it attains a lofty height and a diameter of several feet, and ranks among the largest trees of the north of Europe. Its leaves are broad, of a fine texture, and of a light green colour; in shape, they resemble those of the Black Sugar tree and the Sugar Maple. They are not whitish underneath like those of the Sugar Maple, and when the petiole is broken a milky fluid distils from it, which does not take place in the American species.

The flowers of the Norway Maple are small, yellowish and suspended by pretty long peduncles. The seeds grow in two capsules, which are united at the base, compressed, and garnished with large divergent, membraneous wings. They are ripe in the month of September.

In the winter, when the Norway Maple and the Sycamore are stripped of their leaves, they may still be dis-

Pl. 44.

tinguished by their buds. On the Sycamore the last year's shoots are larger than on the Norway Maple, and the buds are of a yellowish colour, while those of the other species are of a reddish complexion, and are united in groups of three. On the two species of American Sugar Maple, the shoots are still more tapering and slender, and the buds are nearly black.

The wood of the Norway Maple is very white and very fine grained : it is easily wrought, and is employed for nearly the same purposes with that of the Sycamore. Among cabinet-makers in Germany such trees are in request as present agreeable accidental variations in the direction of the fibre, similar to the Curled Maple and the Bird's Eye Maple.

The rapid and beautiful vegetation of the Norway Maple in soils inferior to such as are required by the Sycamore, causes it to be extensively planted in Europe for the embellishment of gardens; for which purpose trees are preferred that develop their foliage early, and shed it late, and that afford through the intemperate season a refreshing shade; all which advantages are united in the Norway Maple.

PLATE XLIV.

Fig. 1, A leaf of half the natural size. A seed of the natural size.

SYCAMORE TREE.

Acer pseudo-platanus. A. *foliis quinque lobis , inæqua-*
liter dentatis subtùs glaucescentibus : floribus subspicatis ,
pendulis.

This beautiful tree is diffused over all the center of
Europe, and abounds especially in Bohemia , Hungary ,
and Poland. It thrives most luxuriantly in moist and
fertile soils, and when expanded to its full dimensions,
it is 60 or 70 feet in height, and 2 or 3 feet in diameter.
Its head is spacious, and its foliage thick. On old trees,
the bark of the trunk is deeply furrowed ; on such as
are less than 6 inches in diameter, it is perfectly smooth.
The leaves of the Sycamore are opposite with long petioles, large, and distinctly divided into five unequal lobes ;
they are of a dark green above , and whitish underneath.
In the heat of midsummer, they are covered with a
very sweet, viscid substance, which is gathered with
avidity by bees. The flowers appear towards the end of
April ; they are small, greenish, and grouped into pendulous clusters from 3 to 4 inches in length. The seed
is in capsules about an inch in length, united at the
base, and terminated by a membraneous wing.

When the Sycamore is fully grown , its wood is fine
grained and susceptible of a brilliant polish. In those
parts of Europe where it is most common , it is in

demand with turners for making-wooden ware. It is used for making violins, and when its grain is undulated, for ornamenting forte-pianos. By the interesting experiments of M^r. Hartig, Grand Master of the forests of Prussia, on the comparative value of different species of wood as combustibles, the Sycamore was found to afford more heat than any other wood of the North of Europe.

For several years past, sugar has been made from the Sycamore, in Bohemia and Hungary. Though the attempt has completely succeeded, it appears certain that the sugar is yielded in a smaller proportion than by the Sugar Maple.

In France and England, the Sycamore is a rare tree in the forests, but it is multiplied in pleasure grounds, on account of its rapid growth, the early developement of its foliage in the spring, and the fine shade which it affords through the summer.

It has been observed in England that the foliage of this tree is less injured than that of others, by the saline vapours wafted from the sea; hence it is chosen for situations exposed to these winds. The justness of the observation I have never had an opportunity of examining.

The Sycamore appears to me to possess no one superior property, which entitles it to preference in the United States, over the Sugar Maple and the Black Sugar Tree; but individuals who wish to possess the species may, I doubt not, obtain seeds, by addressing themselves to the politeness of Col. Steevens , who has it at his delightful seat at Hoboken near New York.

PLATE XLIV.

Fig 2 , A leaf of half the natural size. A seed of the natural size.

Pl. 4

Moose Wood.

Acer striatum.

H. J. Redouté del.

Joly sculp

MOOSE WOOD.

Acer striatum. *A. foliis infernè rotundatis , supernè acuminato-tricuspidibus, argutè serratis : racemis sim- plicibus, pendentibus.*

In the Provinces of Nova Scotia and New Brunswick, in the District of Maine, and in the States of Vermont and New Hampshire, this Maple is known only by the name of Moose Wood : in New Jersey and Pennsylvania it is called Striped Maple. This last denomination, which is preferable as being descriptive, I have thought proper to reject, because it is in use only in a part of the United States whese the tree is rare, and is wholly unknown, in those parts in which it abounds. The name of Moose Wood was given it by the first settlers, from observing that the Moose, an animal now become uncommon in this region, subsisted, during the latter part of winter and the beginning of spring upon its young twigs.

. This tree makes its first appearance near Lake St. John, in the latitude of about 47°. that is to say, a little farther north than the preceding species. In Nova Scotia and the District of Maine, where I have most particularly observed it, it fills the forests. In approaching the Hudson it becomes more rare, and beyond this boundary, it is confined to the mountainous tracts of the Alleghanies, on which it is found, in cold and shaded exposures, along the whole range to its termination in Georgia.

In the District of Maine I have always found the Moose Wood most vigourous in mixt forests, or what are called *Mixture lands;* where the woods are composed of the Sugar Maple, the Beech, the White Birch, the Yellow Birch, and the Hemlock Spruce. In these forests, it constitutes a great part of the under growth; for its ordinary height is less than 10 feet, though I have found individual trees, of more than twice this stature.

The trunk and branches of the Moose Wood are clad in a smooth, green bark, longitudinally marked with black stripes, by which it is easily distinguishable, at all seasons of the year.

This is one of the earliest trees of North America, whose vegetation announces the approach of the genial season. Its buds and leaves, when beginning to unfold, are rose coloured, and have a pleasing effect; but this hue soon changes to green. On luxuriant trees, the leaves are of a pretty thick texture, and finely serrate. They are 4 or 5 inches broad, rounded at the base, and divided into three deep and acute lobes. The flowers are of a greenish cast, and grouped on long, pendulous peduncles. The fruit, which in the main resembles that of the other Maples, is remarkable for a small cavity on one side of the capsules : it is produced in abundance , and is ripe about the end of September.

The inferior size of the Moose Wood forbids its use in any kind of construction ; but as it is white and fine-grained, the cabinet-makers of Halifax , employ it instead of the Holly, which does not grow in so northern a climate , for forming the white lines , with which they inlay Mahogany. Its principal advantage to the inhabitants consists in furnishing them , at the close of winter, when their forage is exhausted , a resource for sustaining their cattle, till the advancing season has renewed the herbage. As soon as the buds begin to swell ; the famished horses and neat cattle are turned loose into the woods, to browse on the young shoots, which they consume with avidity. Poor as this resource may appear, it is not wholly inadequate, since the twigs are tender , and full of saccharine juice. A similar practice prevails, also , in the new settlements of the West.

This species of Maple has been long cultivated in Europe in parks and extensive gardens. It is in request, as one of the earliest trees to feel the approach of spring , but more particularly , on account of the pleasing effect of the white veins , which variegate its trunk. In the primitive forests, where it grows beneath a canopy of impervious shade, these veins are black : the change of colour seems owing to its being planted in drier soils, more open to the sun. Most of the trees of this species , which now grow in Europe , have been grafted on the lofty Sycamore , whose vigor is felt by the Moose Wood , and expands it to four times its natural dimensions.

PLATE XLV.

A branch with fruit of the natural size. Fig. 1 , Bark of a tree in the forests of North America. Fig. 2 , Bark of a tree cultivated on dry and open ground.

Box Elder.

Acer negundo.

BOX ELDER

OR

ASH LEAVED MAPLE.

ACER NEGUNDO. A. *foliis pinnatis ternatisve , inæqualiter serratis : floribus dioicis.*

In the Country west of the Alleghanies , where this tree is common , it is called Box Elder ; east of the mountains it is more rare , and having been less attentively observed , it has received no specific name. Some persons , however , distinguish it by that of Ash leaved Maple , which is a perfectly appropriate denomination : I have chosen the other , though absolutely insignificant of any characteristic property of the tree , because it is sanctioned by general use. The French of Illinois call it *Erable à Giguières.*

The leaves of the Box Elder are opposite , and are from 6 to 15 inches long , according to the vigour of the tree , and the moisture of the soil in which it grows. Each leaf is composed of two pair of leaflets with an odd one. The leaflets are petiolated , oval-acuminate , and sharply toothed : towards fall , the common petiole is of a deep red. The barren and fertile flowers are borne on different trees , and are supported by slender, pendulous peduncles , 6 or 7 inches in length.

Of all the Maples of the United States , this species

ventures least into northern latitudes, for in the Atlantic
States, it is first seen on the banks of the Delaware, in the
neigbourhood of Philadelphia, and even there it is rare.
In the maritime parts of the Southern States, also, it is
far from being a common tree; which is less attributable
to the heat of the summer, than to the marshy nature of
the soil on the borders of the rivers. West of the mountains, on the contrary, it is extremely multiplied, and
instead of being confined, as in the upper parts of Virginia and of the Carolinas, to the river sides, it grows in
the woods, with the Locust, Wild Cherry, and Coffee-
Tree. But in the bottoms which skirt the rivers, where
the soil is deep, fertile, constantly moist, and often
inundated, this tree is most abundant, and most fully
expanded. Even here, it can be considered only as a
tree of secondary size : the largest Box Elders that I
have seen were not more than 50 feet in height, and
20 inches in diameter, and trees of these dimensions are found only in Tennesee and in the back parts
of Georgia, which lie far to the south. In Kentucky
they are of only half this height. Though growing in
thick forests, the Box Elder expands into a head like
that of the Apple tree. I have remarked this form, particularly, on the banks of the Ohio, where I have
also observed that the trunk bulges into knots at unequal distances, and is often decayed at the heart. A fine
row of Box Elders in the botanical garden of Paris,
along the *Rue de Buffon*, affords a sufficiently just

idea of their appearance in the forests, on the Mononghahela and Ohio rivers. It may be concluded from what
has been said, that to attain its full proportions, this
tree requires a climate three or four degrees milder
than that of Philadelphia, Pittsburgh, and Paris.

The Box Elder branches at a small height. The bark of
its trunk is brown, and I have remarked a disagreeable
odour in the cellular integument. The proportion of the
sap to the heart is large, except in very old trees: in these
the heart is variegated with rose coloured and bluish
veins. Some cabinet-makers in the Western Country,
employ it to ornament furniture made of Mahogany or
Wild Cherry Tree. The wood is of a fine and close grain,
and is said to split with difficulty : but as it soon decays
when exposed to the air, it is little used. It has been
erroneously asserted that sugar is made from the sap of
this species.

More than 50 years since, the Box Elder was introduced into France by Admiral La Gallissonière. Subse-
quently, it has spread into Germany and England, where
it is in great request for adorning pleasure grounds, on
account of the rapidity of its growth, and the beauty
of its foliage, whose bright green forms an agreeable
contrast with the surrounding trees. Its young branches,
of a lively green, contribute to the favour in which it
is held, and serve to distinguish it in the winter, when
its leaves are fallen.

The utility of its wood, I believe it has, of late,

been exaggerated; both Europe and America possess many trees superior in strength as well as in size. It appears certain, however, that, growing in copses, and cut every three or four years, it would afford a profitable product in its sprouts, which are very numerous, and which, during the first years, shoot with astonishing rapidity. The success of this experiment will be more certain, if it is made on grounds unfailingly moist and cool; though the Box Elder may seem, for a few years, to prosper in dry and meager soils, it sooner or later pines and perishes. Of this I became convinced in conversing with several proprietors, in the environs of Paris, who, after some recent publications on this tree, had made an unsuccessful attempt to derive profit from their poor lands, by planting them with the Box Elder.

PLATE XLVI.

A branch with leaves and seeds of the natural size.

Mountain Maple.

Acer montanum.

MOUNTAIN MAPLE.

Acer montanum. A. *foliis tri-subquinquelobis, acuminatis, dentatis, rugosis : racemis spiciformibus, suberectis, petalis linearibus.*

This species is more abundant in Canada, Nova Scotia, and along the whole range of the Alleghany Mountains than in any other part of North America. It is called Mountain Maple and Low Maple. Though the last of these names indicates the stature of the tree, I have retained the first, which is more generally in use, and which is likewise appropriate, as this Maple grows of preference on the declivities of mountains exposed to the north, and in cool, moist, and shady situations, on the abrupt and rocky banks of torrents and rivers. On the Mohawk, for instance, near the little falls, it abounds among the enormous rocks which lie scattered along its sides.

The Mountain Maple is 6 or 8 feet in height, and it blooms even at a smaller elevation. It most frequently grows in the form of a shrub, with a single and straight stock. The leaves are large, opposite and divided into three acute and indented lobes : they are slightly hairy at their unfolding, and when fully grown, they are uneven and of dark green upon the upper surface. The blossoms are small, of a greenish colour, and produced in semi-erect spikes from 2 to 4 inches in length. The seeds, which are smaller than those of any other American Maple, are fixed upon slender, pendulous footstalks : they are reddish at their maturity, and each of them is surmounted by a membraneous wing, and has a small cavity upon one side.

The Mountain Maple is too small to be profitably cultivated for its wood, and as its flowers, its roots, and its bark are destitute of any very sensible odour, it promises no resources to medecine. It is found in the gardens of the curious, rather to complete the series of species, than for any remarkable property of its foliage or of its flowers.

This species is commonly grafted upon the Sycamore, and like the Moose Wood, it is thus augmented to twice its natural dimensions. This surprising developement proves how great are the advantages which may be derived from this process and from continued cultivation, in meliorating inferior vegetables.

PLATE XLVII.

A branch with the leaves and flowers of their natural size
Fig. 1, A bunch of seeds of the natural size.

P. J. Redouté del.

Gabriel sc.

Dogwood.

Cornus florida.

DOGWOOD.

Tetrandria monogynia, Linn.   Caprifolia, Juss.

CORNUS FLORIDA. *C. foliis ovalibus , acuminatis , subtùs albicantibus : floribus sessiliter capitatis ; involucro maximo , foliolis apice deformi quasi obcordati; fructibus ovatis , rubris.*

AMONG the eight species of Dogwood which have been observed in North America , this alone is entitled by its size to be classed with the forest trees. It is the most interesting , too , for the value of its wood , the properties of its bark , and the beauty of its flowers. In the United States at large , it is known by the name of Dogwood , and in Connecticut it is also called Box Wood.

The Dogwood is first seen in Massachusetts between the 42° and 43° of latitude , and in proceeding southward , it is met with uninterruptedly throughout the Eastern and Western States , and the two Floridas , to the banks of the Mississippi. Over this vast extent of Country , it is one of the most common trees , and it abounds particularly in New Jersey , Pennsylvania , Maryland , and Virginia , wherever the soil is moist , gravelly , and somewhat uneven ; farther south , in the Carolinas , Georgia , and the Floridas , it is found only on the borders of swamps , and never in the pine barrens , where the soil is too dry and sandy to sustain its vegetation. In the most fertile districts of Kentucky and West Tennessee it does not appear in the forests except where the soil is gravelly, and of a middling quality.

The Dogwood sometimes reaches 30 or 35 feet in height, and 9 or 10 inches in diameter; but it does not generally exceed the height of 18 or 20 feet, and the diameter of 4 or 5 inches. The trunk is strong, and is covered with a blackish bark, chapped into many small portions, which are often in the shape of squares more or less exact. The branches are proportionally less numerous than on other trees, and are regularly disposed nearly in the form of crosses. The young twigs are observed to incline upwards in a semicircular direction.

The leaves are opposite, about 3 inches in length, oval, of a dark green above, and whitish beneath : the upper surface is very distinctly sulcated. Towards the close of summer they are often marked with black spots, and at the approach of winter they change to a dull red.

In New York and New Jersey the flowers are fully blown about the 10 or 15 of May, while the leaves are only beginning to unfold themselves. The flowers are small, yellowish, and collected in bunches, which are surrounded with a very large involucre composed of 4 white floral leaves, sometimes inclining to violet. This fine involucre constitutes all the beauty of the flowers, which are very numerous, and which, in their season, robe the tree in white, like a full blown Apple tree,

and render it one of the fairest ornaments of the American forests.

The seeds of a vivid, glossy red, and of an oval
shape, are always united. They remain upon the trees
till the first frosts, when notwithstanding their bitter-
ness they are devoured by the Robin, *Turdus migra-
torius,* which about this period arrives from the northern
regions.

The wood is hard, compact, heavy, and fine grain-
ed, and is suceptible of a brilliant polish. The sap is perfectly white, and the heart is of a chocolate colour. This tree is
not large enough for works which require pieces of considerable volume : it is used for the handles of light tools
such as mallets, small vices, etc. In the country some
farmers select it for harrow teeth, for the hames of horses'
collars, and also for lining the runners of sledges; but
to whatever purpose it is applied, being liable to
split, it should never be wrought till it is perfectly
seasoned. The shoots when 3 or 4 years old, are
found proper for the light hoops of small, portable
casks; but the consumption in this way is inconsidera-
ble. In the Middle States, the cogs of mill-wheels are
made of Dogwood, and its divergent branches are taken
for the yokes which are put upon the necks of swine,
to prevent their breaking into cultivated enclosures.
Such are the profitable uses of this tree; it affords
also excellent fuel, but it is too small to be brought into
the markets of the cities.

The *liber* or interior bark of the Dogwood is extremely bitter, and proves an excellent remedy in intermitting fevers. It has been known and successfully used
by the country people, as a specific in these maladies,
for more than 5o years. Its medicinal properties were
made the subject of a thesis sustained in the College of
Physic at Philadelphia, in 18o3, in which was presented an analysis of the bark of the Dogwood and of the
Blue Berried Dogwood, compared with the Peruvian bark:
by the experiments made on this occasion, the Dogwood
bark was shown to have a close analogy to the Peruvian
bark, and to be capable, in many cases, of supplying its
place with success. The author of this excellent piece
cites a Physician of Pennsylvania, who, during 20 years,
had constantly employed it, and who estimated 35
grains of it to be equivalent to 3o grains of the Peruvian
bark. The only inconvenience accompanying its use was
that, if taken within a year after being stript from the
tree, it sometimes occasioned acute pains of the bowels:
but this evil was remedied by adding to it 5 grains of
Virginia Snake root, *Aristolochia serpentaria.*

The same author gives a receipt for making an excellent ink in which this bark is substituted for gall
nuts : Put 1/2 an ounce of Dogwood bark, 2 scruples
of sulphate of iron, and 2 scruples of gum arabic, into
16 ounces of rain water ; during the infusion shake it
repeatedly.

The Dogwood merits the attention of Europeans, for

the value of its wood, and especially for the brilliancy of its flowers, by which it is better adapted than almost any other North American tree, to the embellishment of forests, parks, and extensive gardens.

PLATE XLVIII.

A branch with leaves and flowers of the natural size.
Fig. 1, A branch with fruit of the natural size.

GEORGIA BARK.

Pentendria monogynia. Linn.   Rubiaceæ. Juss.

PINCKNEYA PUBENS. P. *foliis oppositis, ovalibus, utrinque acutis; subtomentosis.*

> *Obs.* Floribus majusculis, pallentibus et purpureò-linearibus, fasciculatò-paniculatis. Capsulis subrotundis, modicè compressis : seminibus numerosis, alatis.

THIS tree, still more interesting by the properties of its bark, than by the elegance of its flowers and of its foliage, is indigenous to the most southern parts of the United States : probably its grows also in the two Floridas and in Lower Louisiana. My father found it for the first time in 1791 on the banks of the St. Mary. He carried seeds and young plants to Charleston, and planted them in a garden which he possessed near that city. Though entrusted to an ungrateful soil, they succeeded so well, that in 1807 I found several of them 25 feet high and 7 or 8 inches in diameter; which proves that the vegetation of this tree does not require a very warm climate, nor a very substantial soil.

With a great affinity to the *Cinchona* which yields the Peruvian bark, my father discerned in the Georgia Bark sufficient differences, to distinguish it as a new genus. In testimony of his gratitude and respect, he consecrated it to Charles Cotesworth Pinckney, an en-

Pl. 49.

J. Redouté del.   Gabriel sculp.

Georgia Bark.
Pinckneya pubens.

lightened patron of the arts and sciences, from whom
my father and myself, during our residence in South
Carolina, received multiplied proofs of benevolence
and esteem.

The Georgia Bark is a low tree, dividing itself into
numerous branches, and rarely exceeding the height of
25 feet, and the diameter of 5 or 6 inches at the base.
A cool and shady exposure appears the most favorable
to its growth. Its leaves are opposite, 4 or 5 inches
long, of a light green colour, and downy underneath,
as are also the shoots to which they are attached. The
flowers, which are white with longitudinal rose coloured stripes, are pretty large, and are collected in beautiful panicles at the extremity of the branches. Each
flower is accompagnied by a floral leaf, bordered with
rose colour near the upper edge. The capsules are
round, compressed in the middle, and stored with a
great number of small winged seeds.

The wood of the Georgia Bark is soft, and unfit for
use in the arts; but its inner bark is extremely bitter,
and appears to partake of the febrifuge virtues of the
Cinchona, for the inhabitants of the southern parts of
Georgia employ it successfully in the intermitting fevers
which, during the latter part of summer and the autumn,
prevail in the Southern States. A handful of the bark is
boiled in a quart of water till the liquid is reduced one
half, and the infusion is administered to the sick. From
the properties of its bark the *Pinckneya* has taken the

name of *Georgia Bark*. It is to be wished that some intelligent Physician would examine these properties with care, and indicate with accuracy the manner of employing this indigenous remedy, and the effects to be expected from it : the tree which produces it so nearly resembles the Peruvian vegetable , that some Botanists have included them in the same genus.

PLATE XLIX.

A branch with leaves and flowers of the natural size. Fig. 1, A seed-vessel. Fig. 2, A seed.

Pl. 5

2.

C.J. Bessa del.

Renard sc.

Coffee Tree.

Gymnocladus canadensis.

COFFEE TREE.

Diœcia decandria. Linn.   Leguminosæ. Juss.

GYMNOCLADUS CANADENSIS. G. *foliis bipinnatis, amplissi-
mis, deciduis; foliolis ovalibus, acuminatis. Floribus
racemosis; leguminosis polyspermis.*

UPPER Canada beyond Montreal, and that part of Genesee which borders on Lake Ontario and Lake Erie, are the
most northern countries which produce the Coffee Tree:
but it is much less abundant in these climates than in the
States of Kentucky and Tennessee, and in the tract which
is bounded by the Ohio and Illinois rivers, between
the 35° and 40° of latitude. The large dimensions which
it exibits in these regions is attributable to the milder
temperature of the seasons, and to the extreme fertility of the soil.

The French of Canada call this tree *Chicot;* those of
Illinois *Gros Fevier;* and the Inhabitants of the Western
States, Coffee Tree.

The presence of the Coffee Tree is an index of the
richest lands; on which it habitually grows in company
with the Black Walnut, the Red Elm, the Poplar, the
Blue Ash, the Honey Locust, and the Hackberry. These
trees it equals in height, but not in bulk, for a Coffee

Tree 5o or 6o feet high does not generally exceed 12 or 15 inches in diameter.

In summer this tree when fully grown has a fine appearance : its straight trunk is often destitute of branches for 3o feet, and supports a summit not very widely spread, but of a regular shape and of tufted foliage : such at least is its form in primitive forests, where it is confined by the trees which grow around it. In the winter when its leaves are fallen, the fewness of its branches and the size of the terminal ones, which are very large in comparison with those of other trees, give it a peculiar appearance somewhat resembling a dead tree. This is probably the reason of its being called *Chicot*, Stump tree, by the French Canadians. To this peculiar character is added another of the epidermis, which is extremely rough, and which detaches itself in small, hard, transverse strips, rolled backward at the ends, and projecting sufficiently to render the tree distinguishable at first sight. I have also remarked that the live bark is very bitter, so that a morcel no bigger than a grain of maize chewed for some time produces a violent irritation of the throat.

The leaves are 3 feet long, and 20 inches wide on young and thriving trees : on old ones they are not more than half as large. These leaves are doubly compound, with oval-acuminate leaflets from 1 to 2 inches long. The leaflets are of a dull green, and in the fall the petiole is of a violet colour.

The Coffee Tree belongs to the class *Dioecia* of Linnæus, which includes all vegetables whose barren and
fertile flowers are borne by different plants; in which
case those only that bear the fertile flowers produce fruit:
to effect the fecundation it is necessary that there should
be male plants growing near them. The flowers and the
fruit are large, bowed pods, of a reddish brown colour, and of a pulpy consistency within. They contain
several large, grey seeds which are extremely hard. The
French of Upper Louisiana call them *Gourganes*.

The name of Coffee Tree was given to this vegetable
by the early emigrants to Kentucky and Tennessee, who
hoped to find in its seeds a substitute for coffee : but
the small number of persons who made the experiment abandoned it, as soon as it became easy to obtain from the sea ports the Coffee of the West Indies.

The wood of the Coffee Tree is very compact and of
a rosy hue. The fineness and closeness of its grain fit
for cabinet-making, and its strength renders it proper
for building. Like the Locust, it has the valuable property of rapidly converting its sap into perfect wood,
so that a trunk 6 inches in diameter has only 6 lines of
sap, and may be employed almost entire. These qualities recommend it for propagation in the forests of
the north and of the center of Europe.

The Coffee Tree was sent to France more than 5o
years since. It thrives in the environs of Paris,
where there are there are trees that exceed 4o feet in

height ; but it does not yield fruit, and is multiplied only by shoots obtained by digging trenches round the old trees. The divided roots produce shoots 3 or 4 feet long, the first year. The young trees are sought, on account of their beautiful foliage, for the embellishment of parks and pictoresque gardens.

PLATE L.

A branch with flowers of the natural size. Fig. 1, *A pod of the natural size. Fig.* 2, *A seed of the natural size.*

TABLE.